American Spirit or Great Awokening?

The Battle to Restore or Destroy Our Nation

Bruce D. Abramson

American Spirit or Great Awokening?
The Battle to Restore or Destroy Our Nation

Bruce D. Abramson

Academica Press
Washington~London

Library of Congress Cataloging-in-Publication Data

Names: Abramson, Bruce D. (author)
Title: American spirit or great awokening? : the battle to restore or
destroy our nation | Abramson, Bruce D.
Description: Washington : Academica Press, 2024. | Includes references.
Identifiers: LCCN 2024932334 | ISBN 9781680533385 (hardcover) |
9781680533392 (paperback) | 9781680533408 (e-book)

To the people I love who remain trapped
in Woke jurisdictions and organizations

CONTENTS

FOREWORD

In early 2022, I sat down to write a column on America's spiritual crisis. I thought that it would likely run longer than 800 words. It did. Along the way I benefited from discussions with colleagues at the American Center for Education and Knowledge and at New College of Florida. As I put this project to bed two years later, the topic of academic plagiarism is much in the news. I will thus state affirmatively that everything in this book represents original work. I have, however, presented earlier versions of much of the material. I ran a weekly "American Spirit" series on my "American Restoration" Substack (https://bda1776.substack.com/) through most of 2023. My Woke Soul chapter is an update of "The Trans Movement and the Woke Soul," which appeared in *Human Events*, July 20, 2022. Some arguments, and perhaps even some language, may have appeared in two of my earlier books: *American Restoration: Winning America's Second Civil War* (American Restoration Institute, Kindle Version 2019) and *The New Civil War: Exposing Elites, Fighting Utopian Leftism, and Restoring America* (RealClearPress, 2021).

I. AMERICA'S SPIRITUAL CRISIS

1. Gilded Cages Breed Complacent Slaves

America is suffering from a deep spiritual crisis. Nearly every major movement in contemporary American life—positive or negative, cultural, social, technological, economic, or political—is rooted in our national spiritual vacuum. Modernity has handed us affluence and opportunity far beyond anything that earlier generations could have imagined. We live in delightful, customized cocoons, setting temperature, diet, entertainment, information—and even our bodies—to suit our unique tastes and desires. We are truly blessed.

It has not made us happy. The costs, often hidden, have been incalculable. We live atomized lives, shorn of connection and community, mired in loneliness. We have been given so much that we can think of nothing other than the horrors of having to live without it. We have handed control of our destinies to a nameless, faceless system that claims to speak for a common good while depersonalizing and dehumanizing each constituent individual. We have starved our limbic systems, ignored our deepest needs, driven ourselves into deep, dark anomie. We have become a generation of miserable, pampered, fragile, self-important slaves.

The signs surround us: The skyrocketing rates of alcoholism, drug addiction, obesity, depression, anxiety, mental illness, suicide, child abuse, family dysfunction, and mass shootings all speak to a sickness of the soul. We have fallen, collectively, into an unsustainable abyss. One way or another, we will find our way out of this spiritual crisis. The national polarization that so many miscast as political is truly the tension between two competing spiritual solutions—two ways out of the spiritual morass that point in drastically different directions.

One is Wokeism, a new religion that has arisen to fill our spiritual vacuum. Wokeism speaks most clearly to America's most spiritually-starved people—young, urban, credentialed, professional elites shaping opinion and running institutions. It speaks in their own language and metaphor. It lets them fill their spiritual needs while denying that any such needs exist. It is brilliant, effective, and—as nearly all faiths were in their youth—devastatingly dangerous to adherents and opponents alike.

The other is the American Spirit, a reconnection with our own national spiritual roots. For far too long we—even the most devout among us—have denied their existence. We have seen them as a source of shame, buried them or recast them as embarrassing artifacts of an older time. Yet we need them now, perhaps more than ever. For those of us who have not and do not want to embrace Wokeism, a reconnection with America's founding spirituality marks the only path forward. A reinvigorated American Spirit will allow us to reforge our community, retrieve our connection, restore our nation, and heal our souls.

America was born spiritual. Long before we declared our independence from England, those arriving on our shores saw a new Israel, this bountiful continent as a new promised land. Like the Biblical Israelites—and unlike so many other nations—we recorded our national birth. The Declaration of Independence is a deeply spiritual document. It defined a new nation around a skeletal platform of spirituality and ethics. From birth, America was a welcoming nation eager to absorb the best that the world could offer. Any faith tradition compatible with our skeletal spirituality was welcome to help its adherents become true, full Americans. Many succeeded. Some failed.

This new homegrown Woke faith poses a particular challenge. Wokeism, at least as currently configured, appears incompatible with the American spiritual platform. Perhaps, given time, an American-compatible version of Wokeism could arise. Today's Wokeism is not such a faith. In its present form and along its current trajectory, it cannot co-exist peacefully with the American Spirit.

In many ways, contemporary American Wokeism is forcing us to relearn some of the earliest lessons of the Bible. Consider, for example, a critical short story tucked between Noah and Abraham: The Tower of Babel. If you haven't read the story recently, it's worth revisiting. As one of the two great stories of hubris in the Western Canon (the other is the

Fall of Icarus), the Tower of Babel may be the single most apt allegory for our times.

The story opens in an era of feel-good globalization and harmony. "The whole earth was of one language and of one speech." The people's greatest fear was that divine intervention—for unstated reasons—would leave them "scattered abroad upon the face of the whole earth." To avoid such a terrifying outcome, they devised a unity project: A tower to the heavens.

It's hard to see the problem. Mere generations after a horrendously destructive flood, the people had achieved peace, unity, cooperation, purpose, and a sense of the common good. Their biggest fear was falling back into a state of competition, miscommunication, resource depletion, and disconnection. Hardly the stuff of villainy.

Or so it seems. Their unity project was really a vanity job. Their explicitly stated goal was: "let us build us a city, and a tower, with its top in heaven, and let us make us a name." They built a monument to themselves. Their united purpose was memorializing just how great they were, just how worthy of fame and admiration. In fact, they were almost godlike!

That didn't sit so well with God, who was actually godlike (don't take my word for it; it's in his name). How did God punish them? He handed them their greatest fear. He scattered them, complicated communications, and set them at cross-purposes against each other. He introduced division, separation, and loneliness.

How does that relate to our times? We live in a world whose Woke elite, like the people of Babel, have transcended the parochial constraints of nationalism to take a global view of the problems plaguing humanity. They operate without concern for borders, national identities, or even glitches in communication. They recognize the connections binding us all together and the pitfalls most likely to drag us down.

Working together, they have undertaken challenges that no prior generation would even have considered. They have united to repair the climate, eradicate a virus, and rewrite genetics. Until fairly recently, such tasks had been relegated to the divine—challenges whose resolution existed only in heaven. Not today! Modern brilliance has brought us a class of elite experts so magnanimous, so enlightened, so gifted, that they can reach heights previously reserved only to God himself. They see no downsides. They focus entirely upon their own expertise, their own grandeur, and their deep commitment to the common good. They mock the very idea that some challenges are beyond their human capabilities, some questions inherently unanswerable, some tasks best left to God. The absence of spirituality in their lives is rivaled only by the absence of humility. They embrace Wokeism precisely because its anti-Biblical ethics validate their need for transcendence.

Meanwhile, what is the real scourge of our time? Lack of community. Lack of purpose. Absence of meaning. Anomie. Those are precisely the problems that Wokeism exacerbates—as the Woke embrace of the draconian Covid protocols showed. The provisions did more than merely prove most popular among America's urban, affluent, credentialed, elite. They invigorated the überelite World Economic Forum—whose leadership promotes them as the model of excellent global governance it seeks to roll out broadly and permanently.

In their view, we should count ourselves fortunate to have such a gifted elite. Perhaps they will succeed in building a monument to their own talent. If only they would direct their efforts to the problems that truly plague us as atomized, disconnected humans rather than focusing on the cosmic problems best left to God! Our global elite is intent upon fixing the problems of the globe while exacerbating the problems of humanity. It is not divine intervention that will scatter us; it is an elite that has rejected the ethics of even the most foundational and most clearly universal lessons of the Bible. Spiritual crisis, anyone?

In Biblical ethics, a leadership too taken with its own glory, too focused on building monuments to itself, too committed to impinging upon the realm of the divine, is inviting the demise of the society it claims to lead. A leadership focused on the unachievable in the heavens dooms those of us on earth to the worst fate imaginable: disconnection, loneliness, and deep limbic pain. Today's Woke elite are so committed to their unified encroachment upon the divine that they have eviscerated the basic ethical core at the heart of all Biblically-grounded traditions—including the

American Spirit. In so doing, they have turned us into slaves, subverting our wills and needs to their greater wisdom about the common good. As we learned during Covid, our great ability to customize our environments has rendered such slavery and captivity palatable. Wokeism seeks complacent slaves living in gilded cages. It's hardly even subtle about that desire. In the immortal words of the World Economic Forum: "You will own nothing and you will be happy."

This inherent conflict pitting the American Spirit vs. The Great Awokening thus defines the battle for the American soul—and for the future of our great nation. I, for one, am far from neutral; I side with traditional Americanism grounded in Biblical ethics. I see Wokeism as a false faith grounded in the same anti-Biblical utopian tradition that gave the world communism and fascism. I write in the hope of reinvigorating and redirecting the cultural and political engagement of all American faith communities that embrace our defining national spirit. Our struggle is existential.

Nevertheless, because I see Wokeism as a religion, I treat it seriously and respectfully. It's easy to mock those whose beliefs don't align with our own but derision is a poor way to understand what adherents believe or feel. When I say that Wokeism fills a spiritual vacuum using only contemporary language and metaphor, I'm recognizing that it plays an important defining role in the lives of the Woke. As false and as dangerous as I may believe it to be, I can't access the beliefs of the faithful unless I take their faith seriously.

In fact, one of the goals driving this inquiry is the development of an intellectual framework capable of underpinning a legal argument: The Woke are attempting to turn their faith into the established religion of the United States. Unless we can be honest about what Wokeism is, we will be powerless to stop those efforts.

Another of my goals is the revival of America's spiritual tradition and a reinvigoration of religious involvement in American civic life. In America today, few tradition-oriented religious leaders are effective at reaching beyond their own flocks. They're particularly poor at reaching the urban, credentialed, professional elite. Wokeism, on the other hand, does a great job at reaching those people. Why? Only an understanding of what works can help our traditional faith leaders retool their messaging to reach this critically important audience. This inquiry thus represents my effort to breathe new life into America's faith traditions, catapult them back into a position of cultural influence, and deploy the law to defeat the onslaught of supremacist Wokeism.

2. Lessons of Rejection

Here's a question that most authors should ask but few do: Why listen to me?

Why should anyone care what I have to say about faith? After all, it's not like I'm ordained, or a professor of religion, or a committed activist atheist. Furthermore, unlike a majority of Americans of faith, I'm not a Christian. I'm not even sure that I qualify as a man of faith; I consider all such judgments to be far above my pay grade. What I am is a guy—an American Jew—raised in a traditional Modern Orthodox home and community who walked away from religious observance while still in his late teens and eventually came to question the wisdom of that decision. How does that qualify *me* to write about topics like spiritual crises, America's spiritual roots, or the new religion of Wokeism?

Perhaps it doesn't. Then again, I'm also a guy who always remained deeply connected to his Jewishness and a guy who never stopped trying to understand faith. Perhaps what qualifies me to conduct this inquiry is that I made many poor decisions without ever foreclosing the possibility that I might be wrong. Perhaps what qualifies me is that I've made, in my personal life, many of the errors that I see roiling the country—and certainly, many of the errors that dominate the thinking of my elite compatriots comprising my urban, credentialed, affluent, professional demographic. Perhaps this entire inquiry is possible only because of my history of failure, openness, education, error, and rediscovery. Perhaps my personal spiritual journey is of direct relevance to the critical issue of America's national survival at this very important juncture. Here, then, is my extended *mea culpa*:

My journey began when, as a very intellectual young man, I decided that I did not need a spiritual life. There were many reasons for that rejection. They ranged from philosophical questions about the nature of God, through ethical quandaries about the elevation of religiosity over decency, to practical displeasure with anything that constrained my exploration or my fun. Their combined effect was powerful. I could see many costs and few benefits to remaining within the fold. I kept my interest open but freed my behavior. I walked away.

I was hardly alone in concluding that spirituality was unnecessary. In fact, it is precisely that rejection of spirituality—writ large across the Western world—that is now poised to destroy individual freedom, human dignity, the age of reason, morality, common decency, free market economics, basic societal functioning, liberal values, democratic participation, and republicanism.

I have since come to recognize my error. Spirituality appears to be a basic human need. Denying it as such creates a vacuum that something must fill. That something must arrive in language that speaks to the listener. As a young intellectual, little traditional faith language spoke to me. That's unsurprising. The world's spiritual traditions arose in the pre-modern world, casting their messages to resonate with our pre-modern ancestors. Thus, the world's finest spiritual traditions—crafted and polished over the course of centuries to align their offerings with genuine human needs—suffer from marketing campaigns honed for an audience that no longer exists. Few within their current target markets—we residents of the information age—ever look beyond the dated messaging to assess the quality of their finely-crafted artisanal products. Unmet needs and a rejection of quality form a dangerous combination—a widespread opening for charlatans.

Those charlatans are responsible for much of the large-scale madness we see in today's world—specifically the rapid widespread adoption of internally inconsistent beliefs running counter to empirical reality and impervious to factual refinement. Modernity has found ways to meet spiritual needs without sounding spiritual—hence Wokeism. The result is a slick, hollow, toxic product aligned with contemporary conceits and the needs of cognitive dissonance: A morally destructive set of beliefs, fully accessible to those who insist that they have no spiritual core, that nevertheless meets their spiritual needs.

The path I took from my youthful error to my current understanding is instructive. Contrary to the current Woke propensity for assigning identities to individuals based upon some external assessment of group membership, the only two identities I've ever felt are Jewish and American. I've always felt both identities strongly. In practice, that means that I feel a common bond with every Jew, and a different common bond with every American, that sets them apart from the rest of the global population as "my people." I have responsibilities and obligations towards my people that are distinct from, and greater than, any responsibilities I may have towards humanity at large. Any other "identities" that anyone may attribute to me are illegitimate external assignments. They may provide accurate descriptions—I am indeed short, Caucasian, and male—but they convey very little information about who I am, how I feel, and to whom I may express heightened affinity or obligation.

The Modern Orthodox Judaism in which I was raised immersed me in an environment committed to preserving tradition while embracing modernity. I found many flaws with that environment—not surprising given that I left it as soon as I had the freedom to do so—but that hardly means that I left it behind. From there, I dedicated most of my time to disciplines generally considered non-religious: Computer Science, Artificial Intelligence, Management Science, Economics, Law, Politics, and Public Policy. Along the way, I gained some basic familiarity and comfort with selected elements of Christianity, New Age spirituality and sexuality, Buddhism, Islam, and various other faith traditions. That background colors my interpretations, examples, and references. It has framed my journey, my observations, and the conclusions I have drawn from them.

My youthful abandonment of spirituality made me little more than a young man of my times. According to a recent Public Religion Research Institute poll, a large and growing segment of America now describes its religion as "none." A far larger segment of the country claims a traditional religious affiliation but demonstrates little beyond a rather nominal connection. For the overwhelming majority of Americans—and Westerners—alive today, spirituality is a dead letter. That segment shows a significant overlap with our urban, credentialed, affluent, professional elite class—a class to which I have always belonged. That overlap is hardly coincidental. For many of them—for many of us—it's a point of pride.

In perhaps another sign of our times, I also spent a couple of years immersed in San Francisco's alternative community scene. I was struck at how much those communities had in common with the very traditional religious communities of my youth—and other religious communities of which I'd since become aware. It was as if all these seekers had rebelled against the absurdities they'd found in traditional religions, left them behind, then re-created them in some perverse, mirror-image, form.

It began, as you might expect, with "secret handshakes" and jargon known widely among the initiates but unknown to the world at large. I learned of famous thinkers and writers whose fame had never before reached me—but were indeed sufficiently prominent to have written dozens of books and to command hefty five-figure speakers fees. Incredulous community members would look at me quizzically and ask "Wait! You mean you never heard of...?" using precisely the tone I'd known from *yeshiva* students stunned that most of the world has never heard of history's greatest Torah commentators.

Rituals and community-building exercises abounded. The same people who derided speaking in tongues and snake handling loved ecstatic dancing in a moonlit grove. Those who derided the foolish belief in the rapture committed vast energies to their own apocalyptic beliefs about climate. Regularly scheduled orgies subject to clear rules for admission and participation brought the community together as surely as a Shabbat service or a Sunday mass. Pilgrimages to the "Playa" of Burning Man (or for the less devout, to selected music festivals) were an annual rite. At the Playa itself, carefully laid out maps place an ornately designed wooden "man" and "temple" at the center of everyone's adoration. On the last two evenings, the pilgrims gather to burn first the temple, then the man, in ritualistic fire ceremonies that would have been recognizable millennia ago.

I looked and listened and learned. I embraced my new friends and explored these places that had brought meaning into their lives. I experienced moments of sheer joy and abject horror. Above all, however, I gained a genuine, new, deep appreciation for the community of my upbringing. I observed that, like traditional religious communities, these newly formed alternative communities brought together three types of people: Some were fortunate to have found the only niche in which they could possibly thrive. Some had been trapped through misfortune in a weird little world that was destroying them. Some would have been fine anywhere but chose a niche community that gave their lives particular meaning.

Perhaps more importantly, I found answers to many of the questions that had plagued me through much of my life. For years, I had agonized over the narrow specificity of Jewish law, the insistence on proper language and timing for prayer, the strict adherence to narrow custom and practice, and the insistence that each of these details was precisely correct and deeply meaningful.

I'd found the attention to detail rather silly. Until, that is, I found myself surrounded by people completely unencumbered by such nonsensical religious legal systems and untethered to symbolic rituals—who had created for themselves equally rigid rules and equally symbolic rituals. Watching my new friends, learning their rites, their rules, their rituals, I finally understood that the specifics were far less important than the agreement upon specifics. These seemingly pointless, arbitrary decisions play important roles in human existence. They provide mechanisms for connecting with others, forming communities, and accessing something greater than ourselves.

That observation resonated with my experience in the engineering, economic, and legal worlds. It's irrelevant whether we all drive on the right or the left, as long as we all drive on the same side. The existence of standards is often more important than the substance of those standards. In the spiritual realm, only uniform standards—secret handshakes, jargon, celebrity wisdom, rituals—can define a community of people bound together through time and space. Without such specificity the entire edifice would crumble into untethered individualism. My immersion in New Age communities taught me why the most stringent denominations of Judaism and Christianity thrive while the West's more flexible faith denominations are collapsing.

So many aspects of that immersion proved eye-opening. In the scheme of widely shared communal experiences, a friend once turned to me, shocked, and asked "What do you mean you've never been to a twelve-step meeting?" I replied, "Well, I'm not an addict." "I never knew anyone who's never been to a meeting," she said. I've still not been to a meeting, but I have learned deep respect for the Twelve Steps—and even more, for the marvelous Serenity Prayer—for the power they confer. The alternative communities I experienced taught me that intentional rejection cannot dispense with the human need for reflection, for connection, for surrender, for a higher power. Those who rejected the traditional paths to fulfilling these deep human needs had no alternative but to recreate them in novel, if often perverse, form.

I understood that the people I met in this alternative world were grappling with the consequences of their own rejection—and moving towards creating something that would differ only in specifics from whatever they had fled. Some were not even subtle about it. A sex guru who had become a close friend once confided to a small group of us that she was founding the world's next great religion—derived from her philosophy that female orgasm unlocks the gateway to a primal energy force. "Just what this world needs," I replied. "A new religion." "This one is different," she promised. "It's based on Truth." "Great idea!" I agreed. "I'm just surprised that no one ever thought of *that* before." She withdrew from our friendship shortly thereafter.

The lessons that I learned during my alternative New Age stint alerted me to what was occurring around me. Widespread rejection of our spiritual traditions had led large swathes of America into ignorance, denial, and disconnection. It had created unarticulated needs so shameful that none could speak their name. But the needs were there, nonetheless. People—many far more "respectable" than my San Francisco friends—were casting about for something to meet those needs.

Those of us alive in the 2020s go through our lives mired in denial. We like to believe we live in a world of reason, of science, of technology. While we accept that much remains unknown, we bristle at the idea that there may be a realm of the unknowable. We recoil instinctively at the thought that some sentient deity might reign within that unknowable realm. Those of us who do venture, on occasion, into the spiritual realm tend to do so privately and quietly. For most, the entire concept reeks of superstition and mythology—stories aged relatives from the old country tell children. My desire to rid my life of this nonsense and the burdens that come with it was hardly anomalous. I was but one more young man trying to move beyond a religious upbringing into the more enlightened environs that define modernity.

The commonality of my error, however, does little to mitigate its enormity—or its impossibility. Spirituality, I have come to learn, is a basic human need. It is not a need on par with food or sleep—needs that must be met regularly to sustain life—but it is a need on par with sex. The many New Age tomes on sacred sexuality raise an important point, though likely not the point their authors had hoped to raise.

Like the need for sex, the need for spirit may be denied. In my late teens, when I proclaimed my abandonment of spirit, I could just as easily have declared myself celibate (though that would have been a lot less fun). I could have led a virginal life, a life entirely devoid of sex (again, less fun). What I could not have done (short, perhaps, of self-mutilation) is declare myself free of either a sex drive or a desire to procreate. Yes, I might have learned to control those impulses, perhaps relegating them to a few fleeting moments of unhappiness arising at various points throughout my life. Many have. I could not, however, have extinguished them. They are a natural part of healthy human physical, psychological, and emotional existence—an evolutionary necessity that guarantees the continued existence of the human species. So too with spirituality.

Which brings me back to a critical lesson that I learned repeatedly in the various secular academic disciplines that have occupied much of my learning—and that provides the final answer to the question, "Why me?" You should listen to what I have to say about spirituality and America's spiritual crisis because I'm not a wannabe guru. The applicable critical lesson is simple: diagnosis and prescription are distinct skills.

In times of genuine crisis, the most piercing and prescient analyses of the problems facing society—economic, industrial, governmental, social, or spiritual—invariably come from those on the periphery. Those operating on the inside suffer from (at least) one of two shortcomings. Either they have internalized too many of the assumptions underpinning the conventional wisdom of their environment to notice that some of its fundamentals are no longer true (if they ever were); or they have too great a personal stake in the perpetuation of that conventional wisdom to permit anything that might undermine it. Those shortcomings render meaningful internal critiques nearly impossible. Only those who've been relegated to the periphery are capable of identifying and highlighting the areas most in need of reform.

Far too many outside observers believe that their aptitude at detecting genuine problems qualifies them to pose solutions. Their diagnostic acumen, however, rarely translates into anything other than disastrous prescription. My favorite example of this phenomenon is Karl Marx, whose analyses of 19th century capitalism and the problems plaguing it were vastly superior to those of any of his contemporaries. His prescriptions were disastrous on a scale almost unrivaled in human history.

I have no interest in employing such hubris. When it comes to spirituality, my path has qualified me as an observer, combining enough of a background to process my observations with weak enough fidelity to conventional thinking to overcome its blinding assumptions. That positions me at precisely the periphery most suitable for identifying issues and problems in need of reconsideration and reform.

It does not, however, provide me with any great insights when it comes to proposing solutions. I'm comfortable saying that the spiritual vacuum of modern life has promoted evil. I'm comfortable discussing the mechanisms that made that vacuum possible. I'm comfortable identifying areas in which our finer, God-based, spiritual traditions could benefit from a bit of self-improvement. I'm spectacularly uncomfortable directing traditionalists towards reforms capable of improving receptivity to tradition without undermining the traditions themselves. I emphatically oppose the creation of new religions or sects. We've got plenty of fine choices already on the table, and immature faiths—like Wokeism—are invariably dangerous both to those who embrace them and to those who oppose them.

This inquiry is a call to reinvigorate traditional faiths in ways that bring their timeless spiritual offerings to a modern, anti-spiritualist flock. I'm not the one to effect that reinvigoration. Those efforts must come from within our finest faith traditions and the wisest of the contemporary leaders who stand at their helm. Perhaps by identifying and analyzing the keys to the phenomenal success of Wokeism at speaking to America's spiritually starved elite I can help those traditionalists find ways to mimic Wokeism's messaging success while conveying far more positive, uplifting, and life-affirming messages.

3. Something New Under the Sun

How did our spiritual nation fall into such a spiritual morass? The answer is clear: The times dictated its fall from grace. Not too long ago, human history hit an inflection point. Something shifted. Reality changed.

Modernity is unique. Many things—but far from everything—that had "always" been true stopped being true. The nature of our environment changed; human nature did not. Part of our collective response was an abandonment of traditional faith. Today's West is likely history's most overtly anti-religious society. Many societies have rejected the specifics of the faith their ancestors had handed them. None before ours have rejected the entire notion of faith. It's a unique response that raises a critical question: What makes the modern world unique? Perhaps more pointedly: Why has the Western abandonment of traditional faith become so pronounced over the past few centuries—and accelerated so greatly in recent decades?

Every contemporary faith leader should ponder those questions. None of the cheap answers work. Selfishness, hedonism, materialism, ease, freedom, etc. merely scratch the surface—particularly if you agree that spirituality is a core human need. No, it turns out that there's a genuine dynamic at play that all faith leaders and faith communities must understand: Recent centuries really have marked a discontinuity in human existence.

"What was will be, what's been done will be done, and there's nothing new under the sun." Perhaps. Though it does seem that something new under the sun has arisen to dominate recent existence. From time immemorial, the basic condition of human existence has been scarcity. Industrialization and capitalism ushered in an era of abundance.

It's impossible to overstate the importance of that shift. Until fairly recently, the overwhelming majority of all human activity was dedicated to the production of food. That allocation of effort was hardly frivolous. The overwhelming challenge facing humanity—in all eras, all cultures, and all parts of the world—has been the provision of enough food, with guaranteed consistency, to feed the community. Well fed communities, in turn, then expended considerable efforts securing their food sources, trade lines, and storehouses against the inevitable attacks from poorly fed neighboring communities. And it was not just food. Potable water was at least as scarce (far more so in some parts of the world). Other basic resources posed similar problems. Quality shelter, energy production, clothes, tools, sanitation, medication, safe navigation, and information were equally scarce. Those gifted in producing and securing them could command positions of wealth and honor.

That hardly describes today's world. In fact, we in the 2020s are so detached from that seeming invariant of human existence that when the President of the United States warned of looming food shortages in 2022, most Americans yawned. We simply lack the imagination to appreciate what that might mean.

Today's world has replaced scarcity with abundance. We know how to produce enough food, potable water, shelter, energy, clothing, tools, and medication to meet the needs of more than eight billion people—with no capacity constraints in sight. We have learned how to police the world to ensure the safety of our roads and seas. Information overload now places a premium on the ability to filter unwanted tidbits rather on than the ability to gather new data. That we do encounter occasional localized crises is a function of flawed government policies and problems with distribution. Those are tragic failures—but they are not failures borne of scarcity.

In today's world, too much garbage (i.e., pollution and other undesirable by-products of production) has replaced too little food as humanity's primary challenge. Too much garbage is a very real problem. It is a far lesser problem than too little food.

Great, I can hear you saying. But that's economics. What does it have to do with spirituality? Turns out, the answer is everything. Even a cursory look at any of the world's spiritual traditions shows that God (or gods) fills two primary roles: provider and protector. God is both the ultimate farmer and the ultimate soldier. Even God's more sophisticated tasks—creator, redeemer, avenger, savior, or judge—fit into one of those two categories: A creator is the ultimate provider while the dispensation of true justice is the most genuine form of protection. All of the world's spiritual traditions relate to God's dominance of these two realms. Nearly all traditional sacrifices, prayers, and rituals appeal to the divine within one of these two critical roles.

The shift from scarcity to abundance has eliminated the need for a divine provider. The analogous shift in the lethality of weaponry and the professionalization of policing and military has eliminated the need for a divine protector. Stated simply, today's Americans trust technology, bureaucracy, professionalism, and education to keep them fed and safe. Is that trust misplaced? Is it overplayed? Does it represent the sort of classic hubris that has always led to personal and societal downfall?

Those questions are all secondary. The bottom line is that any American born over the past eighty years who chose to trust human institutions to provide and protect has lived a life charmed by historical standards. Who needs divine intervention when we can provide and protect by ourselves?

That's particularly true among America's elite—the urban, affluent, credentialed, professional classes most likely to have abandoned traditional faiths most fully. The traditional provider/protector god has little to offer them. Divine provision and protection would be redundant, hence unnecessary. What they need is a white-collar god. They live their lives trusting machines, systems, networks, algorithms, authorities, and experts whose inner workings they don't even pretend to understand. They have minimal interest in "popping the hood." Their faith is in the integrity and continued functioning of those delivery mechanisms. Only a god vested in the same place as their faith is capable of speaking to their hearts. What they need is a literal *deus ex machina*—a god of the machine. For many, AI promises the sort of transcendent deliverance traditional faiths assign to a messiah.

Modernity shifted humanity from a world of scarcity to a world of abundance. A new world, understandably, needs new gods. Adam Smith should have provided a wakeup call. Whereas the biblical "strong hand and outstretched arm" freed the slaves, Smith's "invisible hand" shuffled resources to the places best able to use them. Traditional deities bring strength, freedom, and justice. Modern deities work the magic of distribution. Far more than a farmer god or a soldier god, a modernity born of abundance needs a managerial god. Needless to say, few prayers or rituals honed for the pre-modern world address that very modern need (at least directly and literally).

That mismatch created a vacuum. It's easy for contemporary elites to see a provider/protector god as speaking primarily to dated, old world concerns—and thus exclusively to the people mired in them. It's easy for anyone to walk away from a god whose archaic language fails to reach the locus of contemporary faith. It's even easier to walk away from irrelevant rituals and the communities that gather to practice them.

Admonitions of the Psalmist notwithstanding, it's easiest of all to "put your trust in princes and the son of man" who deliver consistent and improving quality. Say what you will about modernity, the quality of life ratchets forward with each passing decade. Modern man lives longer, with fewer maladies, a greater range of experiences, more material possessions, better food, freer sexuality, and far more leisure time, than did any of his predecessors. If modernity's elite provisions are indeed to come to nothing, their demise hardly seems imminent.

The supernatural, however, abhors a vacuum every bit as much as does nature. The ease and comfort inherent in walking away from an unneeded provider/protector god leaves open a critical question: Are those same people also walking away from a god they need quite deeply?

Consider Maimonides' explanation for the copious biblical passages detailing animal sacrifice. Why does God—creator of the universe, liberator of slaves, provider of the Torah—need a good steak? Maimonides' answer is that the sacrifices had nothing to do with God's needs. The sacrifices addressed very human needs. In an era whose overwhelming ethos could not comprehend a deity that failed to demand visible sacrifice, God provided a way to meet that human need. Thousands of years later, as large parts of the world learned to approach the divine through prayer and meditation rather than through sacrifice, the faith traditions—in this case, Judaism—found ways to accommodate the shift in human needs.

Today, religious traditions that demand more than very occasional animal sacrifice have been relegated to small niches. Among the faithful of the twenty-first century, viewed globally, prayer and meditation are far more important mechanisms for accessing and communing with the divine than are animal (or human) sacrifices.

Modernity is thus not the first time that "sophistication" has shifted the dominant human approach to the divine. In keeping with my overall thesis that spirituality—a connection with the realm of the unknowable—is a basic human need, those who have allowed the seeming irrelevance of a provider/protector god to alienate them from the entire concept of the divine have opened a chasm in their lives. Few can find fulfillment with such a gaping hole at the center of their existence. Whether they know it or not, they will expend enormous time and effort looking for ways to fill the needs that they emphatically deny possessing.

That combination of quest and denial screams for exploitation. It creates a market of people seeking something that feels right while refusing the introspection and research necessary to admit that they're even in the market. Charlatans, con artists, and the self-interested will always flock to fill such openings. And that, writ large across our elite class, has become the greatest single threat to the survival of modernity, America, and Western civilization. Our only possible salvation lies in faith—and more, in the few faith traditions that have survived the test of time.

4. The Separation that Defined America

The shift from scarcity to abundance, and the consequent reduction in the importance of a provider/protector deity, defines the primary difference between the modern world and all that preceded it. It is not, however, the only area in which today's West is unique—with American society standing out as the most different of all. Another important area of distinctiveness lies in the separation of church and state—a division so central to the American identity that we enshrined it in the Bill of Rights, then stopped thinking about just how radical it truly is.

Historically speaking, only minority religions ever favored such a separation. "Maybe if we pay our taxes and fly the flag, the King will let us practice our faith in peace" is the sort of thing uttered exclusively by adherents of faiths other than the King's. The relegation of religion to a distinctive set of prayers, rituals, and holidays—effectively reserving large swathes of economic and social life to the state or to the people—is a rather recent and very Western innovation. In trying to understand the spiritual crisis undermining American life today, it's worth taking a bit of a detour to consider the origins of this very American anomaly.

In the parts of the world long dominated by Islam, Hinduism, Buddhism, and Confucianism—as well as what we know about Pre-Columbian Americas and the pagan worlds that preceded Christianity and Islam—no such distinction has ever existed. In some times and places the official religion has been subservient to the state; in others, the state has served the faith. In almost no historical context other than our own has there been a division among clerical, temporal, cultural, and economic spheres sufficiently clean for those controlling one part of society to disregard the concerns and traditions inherent in the others. Even today, in the Muslim-majority world, Islam is far more a way of life than a distinctive set of holidays and prayer texts. The same is true in selected Chasidic enclaves and among groups like the Amish.

The lines among faith, culture, and governance have always been blurred. In Biblical Judaism, God conferred rights and responsibilities on leaders via priests and prophets. When Moses neared death, God told him to ascend to a hilltop, in full view of the people, with the High Priest Elazar and Joshua, "a man in whom is spirit." Once there, God communicated His designation of Joshua as Moses's successor to Elazar through the *urim v'tumim* (the mystical gemstones of the breastplate). Centuries later, when King Saul failed to follow a direct command concerning the eradication of Amalek to the letter, God told Samuel to wrest the royal line from him and hand it to David. The later prophets spent most of their time admonishing the Kings of Judah and Israel—not for failed governance or flawed economics, but for deviating from God's word. Jews did not develop the edict of *dina d'malchuta dina*—the law of the land is the law—until after the Roman decimation of Judea in the wake of the Bar Kochba rebellion in 136 C.E. Only with that concept in place could Jews comfortably obey temporal laws that differed from the prescribed Jewish lifestyle (with only a tiny subset carved out as exceptions).

Of all the world's great faiths, Christianity has taken by far the most interesting and unusual trek down this path. In a story reported in all three synoptic Gospels, Jesus and his followers found themselves accosted by Roman tax collectors. His followers faced a quandary: How could they, in good faith, fund their oppressors? Jesus directed them to look at the coins. Whose face did they see? "Caesar's," they replied. Upon which Jesus taught: "Render unto Caesar what is Caesar's; render unto God what is God's." That much is well known, even among today's anti-religious elites who pride themselves on having never read the Bible (after all, annoying tax collectors remain highly relevant in modern life). What is less well known, even among the biblically literate, is the line that follows—the line revealing how this wisdom was received. The people who heard it "marveled" at its wisdom. Contrary to our contemporary conceit that the division between church and state is obvious and clear, the thought was far from mundane to those who walked with Jesus two millennia ago. Obey two distinct sources of authority in two different aspects of life? How radical!

That message served early Christianity quite well during its three-plus centuries as a despised, discriminated against, minority faith. It did not, however, survive Christianity's transition to the official religion of the Roman Empire. Almost as soon as Constantine adopted Christianity, he convened the Council of Nicaea to canonize his new faith; Christianity could hardly be the official faith of the Roman Empire without an official Roman Christianity. Whereas there had been hundreds of gospels, dozens of philosophies, and numerous ways to live as a good Christian prior to the Nicene Creed, the official imperial Christianity labeled most of them heresies. The Roman Church purged most of them from imperial Roman lands, then proved even less generous toward non-Christian faiths. The Church also devised, adopted, and imposed Christian views of society and economics that eventually gelled into the feudal system. By the early Middle Ages it was effectively impossible to tell where Christianity ended and "normal" European life began.

Though non-Roman Christianity survived to the Empire's south and east, Medieval Christendom defined a way of life just as thorough as did Medieval Islam. Even the Great Schism of 1054 did little to alter the all-encompassing nature of Christianity. It merely divided a Western belief in Church primacy over the Crown from an Eastern belief in the primacy of the Crown. The idea that the schism involved solely theology, as opposed to a mixture of theology, politics, economics, and culture, is unsustainable. Christian governance defined all aspects of life.

That all-encompassing definition began to change only with the Reformation—and didn't really take hold until the mid-seventeenth century. For the first time since the Nicene Creed, Protestantism reintroduced to Europe the idea that there are multiple ways to live a Christian life. Needless to say, that idea didn't sit well with the Catholic Church, the incumbent Christian monopolist. Its bloody Counterreformation sought to reimpose the unity not only of faith, but also of culture and society. The resulting stalemate locked in place multiple Christian denominations. Though many of them were established local majorities, every Protestant ruler understood that his own denomination represented a minority faith within Europe. The Catholic Church understood that, its plurality notwithstanding, it lacked the dominance to enforce its will.

The Treaty of Westphalia of 1648 was a multi-denominational agreement among Christian rulers who understood something that minority faiths had long appreciated: If you want to protect your co-religionists (technically, co-denominationalists) living as minorities in other kingdoms, you'd best reciprocate by recognizing the rights of selected minorities living within your own borders.

The mid-seventeenth century European recognition that religious tolerance might buy peace necessarily opened parts of society to differences of practice. When ported to the Americas, the various denominations became even more intertwined. It became clear to all that the only alternative to an even bloodier reprise of Europe's still-recent religious wars was an ironclad guarantee of the Westphalian principle.

As luck would have it, the American founding also happened in a time and place in which religious fervor had cooled (at least compared to what it had been in Europe 150-200 years earlier). Religion as a way of life, however, had hardly evaporated. The many Protestants, the fair number of Catholics, and the small number of Jews comprising the population of England's thirteen colonies lived in a culture deeply rooted in Biblical morality and the behavioral practices of Christian Europe. Fortunately for the Jews, the dominant strand of American Christianity was an Old Testament Protestantism that saw America as the New Israel—a promised land, a shining city on a hill.

By 1776, the forbearance that Europe's exhausted rulers were willing to show towards other Christian denominations in 1648 had expanded enough to encompass America's Jews. As George Washington stated clearly in his 1790 letter to the Jewish community of Newport, Rhode Island: "It is now no more that toleration is spoken of, as if it was by the indulgence of one class of people, that another enjoyed the exercise of their inherent natural rights. For happily the Government of the United States, which gives to bigotry no sanction, to persecution no assistance requires only that they who live under its protection should demean themselves as good citizens, in giving it on all occasions their effectual support." No better description of the American spiritual platform has ever been written. America demands a basic, shared, core moral underpinning from all of its citizens. How those citizens decide to complete their spiritual frameworks beyond that core is up to them.

America's founders crafted a lowest-common-denominator "Deist" civic religion, grounded in Biblical morality, broad enough to encompass every denomination of which they were aware and more than a few to which they had given little or no thought. They then locked their adopted faith in place—as had every other ruler throughout recorded history—with a commitment to avoid "establishing" a national church that might add controversial specifics.

The Declaration of Independence opens with references to God and a Creator. The notion of natural law, or "Nature's God" is inherent in its creedal pronouncement "that all men are created equal, that they are endowed by their Creator with certain unalienable Rights, that among these are Life, Liberty and the pursuit of Happiness." Because it sees governments as "instituted among men," its follow-up document instituting a government—the 1789 Constitution—required no such divine references. But that government became possible only after it was grounded in natural law—and its legitimacy rested entirely upon its fidelity to natural law: "[W]henever any Form of Government becomes destructive of these ends, it is the Right of the People to alter or to abolish it, and to institute new Government."

Like all creeds, this one was aspirational. No one believed that it described reality; it set a goal towards which the members of the new nation had to march. At inception, the contradiction of an equality-based yet slaveholding nation was lost on no one. The early recognition of the impracticality of stamping out slavery while still uniting the colonies fooled no one into believing that slavery was a permanent presence.

The Declaration put American society on warning that the ancient, widespread, and time-tested institution of slavery was on its last legs. The Constitution and some of the country's earliest legislation marked steps towards its ultimate demise less than a century later. Over time, as new cultures came into contact with this American ideal, they too have had to reconcile some longstanding practices with this American creed.

America, however, was born as a big tent—not as a free-for-all. Like all creeds and all nations, America can, should, and must insist that all who seek its shelter—as citizens, residents, or guests—adopt its covenant.

What made America different was that, from inception, its covenant was intentionally incomplete—a point to which Washington's letter alludes. It's hardly coincidental that Thomas Jefferson—the Declaration's primary author and one of the less devout founders—edited the Gospels to eliminate the miracles and leave only the ethics. The notion that Jesus may have been a less-than-divine moral force—a reformist Rabbi railing against the corruption of the authorities of his time—would have been considered heretical through much of Christian history. In America, Jefferson's critical point was that *even if* Jesus were less than divine, he taught many lessons worth learning and internalizing.

Nothing in America imposed the view that Jesus *was* less than divine. His divinity, and the nature of that divinity, defined questions over which good Americans could disagree without running afoul of the civic religion or natural law. His ethical teachings, however, were beyond reproach. What's more, because there is significant overlap among the core ethical teachings of most of the world's great faiths, an American civic religion grounded in Christian ethics was indeed broad enough to encompass not only Judaism (deeply within the consciousness of the founders), but also most other faith traditions far from their thoughts at the time. It was easy enough for adherents of multiple denominations of many faiths, in Washington's terms, to demean themselves as good citizens.

Far from creating a spiritual void, America's founding faith represented a spiritual platform emphatically available to all who sought to build upon it. Different denominations could complete the structure in different ways as long as they did not run afoul of some basic ethical precepts. As for those who rejected those ethical precepts—many of which were enshrined in American law? The law would seek ways to grant exemptions but reserved the right to override religious practices deemed entirely incompatible with basic American ethics. Believers still incapable of embracing those ethical underpinnings faced a choice: They could live as criminals in America or relocate to whatever part of the world was willing to accept their practices. Such a choice is hardly enviable. Nor, however, is it atypical. The American system was designed to be robust enough to accept a dizzyingly wide array of religious practices. It was not designed to be a free-for-all.

Perhaps even more importantly, America's founders recognized that their new civic religion was intentionally incomplete. Religious institutions, traditions, practices, rituals, holidays, theologies, and approaches to spirituality were necessary to complete the package. For those Americans who chose to distance themselves from religious traditions, the institutions of civil society would play that role. That founding civic religion defines the American Spirit.

It's hardly a coincidence that Alexis de Tocqueville, the most important outside observer of the early American nation, recognized that these intermediating institutions played a uniquely important role in American life. Nor is it a coincidence that both Christianity and Judaism have assumed a different complexion in America than they have elsewhere. The American formulation combining a shared ethical civic foundation with widely varied denominational specifics gave rise to an entirely new formulation of religion.

This radical American system shattered the age-old formula in which faith encompassed all aspects of life. It severed basic elements of society, economics, culture, and bedrock morality from the rituals, prayers, holidays, and ethical nuance defining man's relationship with the unknowable or divine. It divided control of the former set between the government and the people while disavowing both national ownership and monopolistic control of the latter set.

That division, which has served our nation and the world so well in so many ways, paved the way towards our anomalous mindset. In the American—and Western—mind, words like religion now correspond solely to the particularistic elements over which our founding documents relinquished all claims. That mindset has complicated many of our interactions with cultures and faiths that adhere to the more traditional and common mindset drawing no such distinction. It has also—and this point is central to understanding our current spiritual crisis—complicated our interactions with ideologies that, despite eschewing any claims to faith, religion, or the divine, are nevertheless as comprehensive as every traditional religion.

America's greatest struggles over the past two centuries have been against comprehensive systems seeking to undermine either our bedrock spiritual morality or the division that has allowed multiple belief structures rest upon that ethical foundation. Ironically, it is precisely our cherished separation of church and state that has made us most vulnerable to such attacks. We are incapable of understanding that just because we have relegated certain activities to the realm of the secular doesn't mean that other cultures, grounded in other faith traditions, share our categorization. The entire notion of "Islamic finance," for example, had to arise because in commerce among Muslims, the charging of interest is not at all "merely economics." It is a core ethical belief about the appropriate relationship between those so blessed with surplus resources that they can lend some out and those who find themselves in a moment of need. Viewed through that lens, finance becomes an integral component of faith-as-a-way-of-life.

A direct corollary of this vulnerability is that by pulling large swathes of economic activity and social organization outside the realm of faith, we've made the remaining parts of faith far more disposable. Societies cannot long function without rules for exchange. Societies can last far longer without prescribed prayer. Where the two remain married, commercial activity anchors even the least devout within a faith system— effectively providing them with a way of meeting spiritual needs as they arise. Where, as in today's West, clear lines are drawn between them, full commercial and social lives become possible untethered to faith, community, ritual, or tradition. Those living seemingly full lives exclusively on the secular side of the divide have nowhere to turn when their spiritual needs call. That makes them easy prey for charlatans—like Marxists, the Woke, or other utopians—who seek to undermine everything the American system has built. Only a recommitment to the American Spirit and traditional faith can thwart their plans.

5. A Big Tent is not a Universal Shelter

At the time of the American founding, the ethics-based American spiritual platform appeared broad enough to be nearly universal. But every ethical principle, by definition, excludes those who contest it. In the nineteenth century, a new strand of Western thought arose to challenge Biblical ethics, and thus the core ethical foundations of the American nation. Wokeism—the great contemporary challenge to America's ethical foundations—is but the most recent ideology to emerge from this still-young tradition.

The uniqueness of the American approach to faith was evident before the founding of the American nation; it became even clearer after the Bill of Rights enshrined it in constitutional law. America's faith communities, first Christian then Jewish then all others, differed from those planted elsewhere. That was particularly true for denominations that had flourished primarily when and where they were dominant. Established faiths can blur the distinctions among religion, governance, economics, and culture. In America, faiths and communities dominant and established elsewhere had to determine which elements of their familiar cultures and lifestyles were central to their faith and which were not. They then had to graft their most important particularistic elements onto the American spiritual platform while relinquishing control over many of the others. That adaptation task was necessarily easier for some denominational communities than for others. A big tent is not a universal shelter.

Not long after the American founding, a new ideological movement seized hold of some of the West's greatest thinkers: Utopian Socialism. Though utopian socialists have long rejected the "religion" label, their primary argument has been that their holistic ideologies seeking to rewrite all aspects of life, community, economics, government, and belief eliminate the need for religion altogether. In other words, their rejection of the "religion" label stems entirely from their dismissal of the concept of a deity and their refusal to acknowledge spirituality as a basic human need. In all other respects, the systems they've sought to construct have been every bit as complete as the most rigidly enforced established faiths. Subsequent experience in states adopting strong-form utopian socialist agendas—the Soviet Union, North Korea, Nazi Germany, and Mao's China come readily to mind—demonstrate clear parallels to rigid theocratic rule. In particular, the wars these regimes waged against disapproved faiths—typically labeling adherents as enemies of the state, of the people, of progress, and/or of justice—highlights their true nature. To insist that such all-encompassing ideological systems are "not religions" is to get caught in semantics. Any system that dictates belief and behavior deserves to be considered and treated as a faith tradition.

Attempts to graft utopian socialist denominations onto the American spiritual platform always posed unique challenges. The utopian socialist writers—with Karl Marx proving to the most influential of the bunch—represented the first significant Western intellectual movement to reject the Biblical tradition since St. Augustine. The centrality of the Biblical tradition to the American founding guaranteed that conflict was inevitable.

At its core, utopian socialism rejects the fall of man. As the Bible's second story (following only creation) the centrality of the fall to both Judaism and Christianity is clear. So too is its message: Humans are flawed; perfection belongs only to God. Rules, laws, rituals, prayers, edicts, and the rest can help improve individual behavior and elevate societal structures, but we humans can never attain perfection. Moreover, the struggle is constant. The moral successes of one generation are not heritable; each generation must refresh them and improve upon them.

That belief is far from unique to Jews and Christians. Islam tells a somewhat different story about the origins of both humanity and evil, but it's at least as adamant that perfection is possible only in unity with God. Hinduism and Buddhism have very different views of life and afterlife, but the suffering inherent in all versions of *samsara* relegates perfection to a different plane of existence. All traditional faiths agree that perfection is effectively unachievable for the living—who must struggle to preserve decency, to connect to higher principles, and to focus on self-improvement in the face of constant challenges. Religious guidance thus provides a path to incremental improvement in this life and elevation in the afterlife.

At a deeply meaningful core level, every major faith tradition that predated the American founding accepted actions and incentives, rules and rituals, beliefs and behaviors, as necessary to elevate the individual and the community above our base animal instincts. Incorporating that fundamental—seemingly near-universal—idea into an American spiritual platform could hardly have been less controversial.

Until, that is, someone made it controversial. Utopians believe in the perfectibility of both humanity and human society. While they may differ among themselves on specifics, they tend to agree that the biggest challenges we face stem not from flawed, animalistic, human instincts but rather from the exploitative aspects of human societies. Perfect society first; human perfection will follow. Even better! Once humanity experiences such perfection, the world will never fall from grace.

Utopian socialism was thus a radical departure not just from the Christianity against which it rebelled explicitly, but from a longstanding near-universal concept of humanity. The strength of that rebellion became possible because utopian socialism was also uniquely attuned to its times. Unlike every faith tradition that preceded it, utopian socialism is unencumbered by scarcity. An ideology typically viewed as a backlash against industrialism was, by its very nature, acutely aware of the fundamental changes that industrialism had wrought. Nineteenth century utopian socialism arose as the world's first ideology anchored in a world of abundance.

In a mindset that cuts across much of the utopian literature and reaches its cleanest, most powerful explication in Marx, abundance is an assumption. It is not, however, a coherent assumption. Utopian socialists tend to believe that resources, growth, production, and innovation are all finite. They tend to describe the constant destruction and recreation of the modes of production as "unsustainable." They worry deeply about resource depletion, the undesirable by-products of production (i.e., pollution), and "the limits of growth." They exert considerable effort searching for ways to curtail that depletion and production before we hit those limits.

At the same time, they also argue that we don't need unrestrained production and growth because we already have enough of everything to meet reasonable demand. We have enough food to feed the world— perhaps not as everyone would like to be fed, but more than enough to sustain life. We have enough water, shelter, energy, communication capacity, transportation bandwidth, material goods, engaging experiences, and leisure time to go around. The remaining challenge is to get those things to the people who need them—in other words, distribution. "From each according to his ability, to each according to his needs" is a profound statement of morality. It is, however, a decidedly nontraditional morality. It is a morality grounded in abundance rather than in scarcity.

The distinction is not hard to see. In a world of scarcity, morality must emphasize constant improvement, growth, production, and protection. Without a unified communal striving in those directions, society will necessarily suffer from starvation, deprivation, infighting over resources, disunity of purpose, and ultimately collapse.

In a world of abundance, morality must emphasize conservation and distribution. Without conservation, society will deplete its resources and suffocate itself with pollution. Without distribution, parts of society will fall back into scarcity. Moreover, having reached the state of sustainable abundance and equitable distribution, the impetus for further growth and improvement will evaporate. The goal will become sustenance. Societal perfection will have been achieved by definition—a perfect society is one in which no further improvement is possible. From there, individuals cursed with the ancient ambitions fueling reckless innovation and growth will stand out as antisocial. Justice and the common good will demand their removal.

Utopianism, socialism, and Marxism are thus emphatically moral systems that speak to people grappling with the challenges of abundance. Because of that orientation, however, their moral codes are deeply at odds with those of Judaism, Christianity, Islam, Hinduism, Buddhism, most other traditional faiths—and America's spiritual platform. Unlike traditional faiths that can—at least in theory—graft their particularistic elements concerning the relationship between adherents and the divine onto the American ethical core, this new utopian tradition challenges that core. It is thus unsurprising that all strong-form denominations of utopian socialism have proved to be deeply and irredeemably anti-American. Contemporary Wokeism falls into that pattern quite cleanly: Its rejection of America's founding as an immoral act speaks clearly to the incompatibility of the Woke moral code and the American Spirit.

Yet, perhaps ironically, many denominational ideologies emerging from this new utopian moral tradition—including Marxism—do share an important element with America's spiritual platform. They accept the distinction Jefferson helped draw between ethics and faith. Whereas the American system deployed that distinction to impose a common ethical core while freeing individuals to follow their own spiritual paths to faith, many utopians reject the idea that their ethical systems might be incomplete and in need of faith.

Utopian socialists thus make the same mistake I did in my youth, the same mistake that has now come to dominate America's affluent, credentialed, professional elite: They conclude that spirituality is unnecessary. They then take the error further: Because spirituality is unnecessary, it is a dangerous impediment on the path toward perfection. Marxists—and many of their fellow utopians—thus seek to eliminate society's spiritual component entirely, relegating faith, rituals, practices, and gods to the dustbin of history.

Marxism failed for many reasons. Much has been written about the lack of realism built into its assumptions about economics and sustainability, its prescriptions for planning, its weak understanding of human nature, its inattention to incentives, and the coercion necessary for equitable distribution. Far too little attention has been given to the ways in which the Marxist rejection of faith renders it an inherently incomplete system. Marxism is simply incapable of meeting the spiritual needs of humanity. Denying that such needs exist is hardly the same as obliterating them. The Marxist view of the spirit, the divine, and the unknowable was ultimately unsustainable.

Antonio Gramsci was among the first important Marxists to notice the spiritual shortcoming at the heart of his faith. His writings gave birth to cultural Marxism, relegating the original to economic, or class-based Marxism. Later scholars broadened the analysis further, generalizing Marxism into Critical Theory. Whereas Marx reduced history to the struggle among economic classes, Critical Theorists reduce history to struggles among rigidly defined groups. Marx contended that the resource-owning class sought uniform control and exploitation of the worker class. Critical Theorists pitch all important historical developments as attempts by an exploitative or oppressor group to impose structural constraints on exploited or oppressed groups. Different critical theorists can then explore different aspects of that exploitation. In its best-known contemporary application, Critical Race Theory (CRT) casts history in terms of an exploitative "white" class oppressing the downtrodden "people of color."

Critical Theory is thus far broader, and potentially much richer, than the original class-based Marxism. Its exploration of struggles based beyond economics offers ways to address human needs, desires, and curiosities arising far from the material realm. A brilliant late twentieth century innovation called "intersectionality" tied its pieces together: All the struggles that Critical Theorists have identified are merely manifestations of a single struggle—a unity that many faith traditions would recognize. Intersectionality began the process of canonizing, unifying, and giving coherence to the official, recognized, legitimate struggles of Wokeism—while rejecting the heretical false consciousness of those who persist in elevating struggles falling outside the canon (essentially the task Constantine assigned the Council of Nicaea).

To the Woke, all non-intersectional conflicts represent little more than infighting among the members of the exploitative class. Thus, most famously, though European antisemitism may have been exploitative, brutal, cruel, and longstanding, it was merely white-on-white crime of minimal significance to the struggle for justice. To Critical Theorists, the obsessive focus on the Holocaust is a ploy to divert attention from the historic struggles of the moment. Too bad for the exterminated Jews and all, but a diversionary sideshow in the scheme of things. The clear and definitive determination of those charged with establishing the intersectional canon is that Jews are an oppressor class. Antisemitism thus is not and cannot be part of the true intersectional struggle.

With intersectionality in play, every existing institution, organization, or tradition must—by necessity and definition—have been put in place by some victorious element of the exploitative class to lock its victory in place. Everything ever used to structure society, from the nuclear family upward, is inherently exploitative.

Intersectionality untethered all who embraced it from fidelity to anything. It created a blank slate ideal for a transformative rebirth—a new tradition beholden to nothing that preceded it. The early twenty-first century is experiencing that birth in the guise of Wokeism.

In short, the world's various faith traditions built societies around comprehensive views melding the spiritual and physical realms. The American system experimented with an incomplete ethical core that only a spiritual tradition could complete. Marxism insisted that completeness required only a systemic approach to the material world. Critical Theory generalized Marxism in ways capable of filling its many gaps. Wokeism has arisen to meld spiritual and cultural components onto Marxism's economic core.

Meanwhile, the American system has changed since inception. Successive generations have pushed faith traditions to the very periphery of American life. Laws misconstruing the Bill of Rights' prohibition on "establishing" a religion have rendered discussions of spirituality toxic; those resting in recognizable faith traditions (particularly Christianity) have been deemed unfit for public airing. In today's America, rituals, customs, practices, symbols, and even ideas associated with traditional faiths enjoy far weaker protection and far less respect than do those grounded in almost any other source. Witness the many public lands that would never allow a Christian shrine to a martyred Jesus but gush over their new Woke shrines to a martyred George Floyd. Or, in a somewhat weaker sense, consider the large swathes of retail in which the Pride Month of June boasts far bigger and far more targeted displays than the traditional year-end Christmas Season. The latter has become controversial for its religious particularism; the former is beyond reproach, with any who dare question its garish displays immediately branded hateful.

America is following the utopian lead of jettisoning the spiritual realm and seeking completeness instead in a code of ethics—at precisely the moment that utopians are broadening their purview to meet the unspoken spiritual needs of their flocks. It would be hard to find a better recipe for allowing an American spiritual crisis to slide into the nation's demise.

Confounding matters even further, the Critical Theoretic positioning of exploitation and struggle at the center of history is overblown, not wrong. Class struggles, race struggles, sex differences, religious battles, tribal wars, and many other fights between groups who see themselves as distinct have indeed shaped much of world history. Today's struggle for the soul of America has a very clear—and very rational—class bias.

Traditional American ethics, like the Biblical ethics from which they grew, are grounded in scarcity. Utopian ethics are grounded in abundance. Coloring today's ethical divide is the obvious distinction between richer and poorer economic classes. Among Americans concerned with recent, present, or foreseeable future scarcity, traditional biblically grounded American ethics remain popular. Among the American elite so mired in abundance that scarcity is almost unimaginable, the utopian Woke ethical code is skyrocketing. Countless polls and studies show that neither ethical code alone brings fulfillment or contentment to its adherents. Those desirable spiritual states require spiritual connections as well as ethical positioning. The spiritual vacuum is very real and very dangerous.

6. Our House Divided

America is a house divided against itself. Our debates have transcended public policy and moved into the realms of meaning and value. We no longer agree about basic terms of discourse: Man, woman, sex, racism, antisemitism, peaceful, freedom, security, misinformation, authoritarian, recession, insurrection, fascism, supremacism, and so many other words long considered self-explanatory have been deconstructed to the point of meaninglessness. Today's America lacks a consensus about even such basic notions as good and bad.

A healthy nation must have a unified vision, mission, and purpose. The American nation was founded with history's finest mission statement: "We hold these truths to be self-evident, that all men are created equal, that they are endowed by their Creator with certain unalienable rights, that among these are life, liberty and the pursuit of happiness." For more than two centuries, people of the world have looked to America as the beacon of liberty.

We have lost that unifying vision. The political shift from Bush to Obama to Trump to Biden has whipsawed American law and policy. We've gone from a country in which we feared that our political opponents would enact expensive, ineffectual plans to one in which we fear that our political opponents will transform America into a country in which we would not want to live.

How did our political struggles become existential? How can those of us who still embrace America as the greatest nation made by man prevail? How can we restore the values that made America exceptional and great? How can we revive the full glory of the American Spirit?

We must begin by confronting the true nature of our malady: Our relegation of spirituality to the outermost periphery of national consciousness has given rise to nearly every prominent element of modern American life—positive or negative, cultural, social, or political. A new Woke religion grounded in the utopian tradition—rather than in the Biblical tradition—has arisen to fill the vacuum.

Wokeism has quickly become the dominant faith of our elite—the urban, affluent, credentialed, professional classes who control our most important institutions. Left unchecked, Wokeism will undermine both the American nation and the American republic. Only a reconnection to the spirit of America's founding—and a reintegration of our traditional faiths into the national fabric—can save us.

What does that mean in practice?

The widespread rejection of traditional religion and of God has created a spiritual vacuum. Many of the basic human needs that history's faith traditions rose to address now go unmet, unrecognized, and even unspoken in modern life. Our proudly anti-religious elites are screaming for spiritual fulfillment while shunning anyone who approaches them speaking a spiritual language. They are lost, wandering, and seeking meaning.

The language and metaphor giving life to traditional religions is unlikely to speak to them. It's hardly coincidental that King David, the Psalmist who wrote "the Lord is my shepherd," was raised as a shepherd, from a family of shepherds, in a community of shepherds. When we first meet the character, the prophet Samuel cannot find David among the many impressive sons of Jesse because the boy is literally "with the sheep." No wonder that even in his royal days, David took comfort in the thought of a divine shepherd!

Shepherding plays less of a role in modern life and occupies less space in the modern psyche. Pastoral metaphors fall flat in places like New York City, Silicon Valley, Washington, DC, and Hollywood. A deity who works with sheep is unlikely to impress investment bankers and neurosurgeons. They need a faith that speaks their language, that relates to their concerns, that aligns with their self-images. They need a faith that can fulfill their spiritual needs without ever forcing them to admit that they have spiritual needs.

Wokeism fits that bill perfectly. Wokeism speaks directly to a flock that is younger, better credentialed, more affluent, more professional, and far more likely to name their religion as "none" than is the overall American population. It appeals largely to those who deride traditional faiths as obsolete superstitions. It manifests itself throughout American leftist culture and politics, most prominently in apocalyptic climate change, Critical Race Theory (CRT), Covid alarmism, the Trans movement, redistributive economics, and cancellation. It's a supremacist movement eager to impose its Truths. Towards that end, it allies with the decidedly non-Woke supremacists of Islamism and the Chinese Communist Party. As a utopian movement that rejects both the Biblical narrative and Biblical morality, Wokeism is antagonistic towards Christianity and Judaism—as well as towards Christians and Jews. Many of Wokeism's basic precepts are antithetical to both the American vision of liberty and all traditional faiths.

Wokeism, however, is not great about defining its terms. Many Woke definitions are amorphous and laden with jargon. The Woke wield deconstruction as a potent weapon, seizing upon words that evoke deep sensation—positive or negative—and redefining them to suit Woke tastes. The Woke typically accuse all who question their vagueness and deconstructions of acting hatefully or of inciting violence. It thus falls upon outside observers to brave the defamations, tease definitions, and extract categorizations from worked examples. In a very real sense, any inquiry into Wokeism is an exercise in definition.

To begin with perhaps the most strategically important of definitional challenges, the Woke insistence that Wokeism is not a religion has let them take great strides towards turning it into something that has never before existed: The established religion of the United States. This onslaught is possible only as long as we allow the Woke to hide the true nature of their faith. Once identified and defined properly, the First Amendment's Establishment Clause can provide much of the protection we need.

In the meantime, Wokeism has made great strides towards that establishment. Few people yet appreciate how the March 2020 Covid lockdowns changed the world—or the role they played in Wokeism's ascent. Part of the blindness stems from cognitive dissonance—again, strongest among our elite. When the lockdowns were first announced, they commanded a global supermajority. Many otherwise rational people were so scared of this new virus that they were willing to suspend their reason, believe that the government would relinquish its emergency powers in fourteen days, and expect that everything would soon return to normal. America's elites, who see themselves as far smarter than the masses, can never admit that they were fooled so completely on a matter of such import.

As those in the minority not blinded by the initial panic understood, however, the lockdowns represented an intentional decision to unravel the entire socioeconomic fabric of Western civilization. That fabric had long been fraying, a clear casualty of America's spiritual crisis. Over the course of decades, more and more Americans had stopped believing in anything. Family, community, country, and God—the greatest sources of meaning throughout recorded history—had all become options or negatives. Americans had lost touch with the American Spirit, lost touch with their own spiritual traditions, lost touch with the source of inalienable rights, and devalued the rights themselves. Only within such an environment was it even thinkable to relegate human rights to dispensations that the government could withhold or grant as it (in its infinite wisdom) deemed appropriate and necessary to serve the common good.

The lockdowns buried the very idea that had animated America's founding. By the end of March, not a government—or even an opposition leader—on the planet was willing to stand and shout that inalienable rights could not be alienated legitimately, even in the case of a panicked populace.

With the American idea thus buried, America's spirituality in deep retreat, and the fabric of society unraveled, it became clear that something new would emerge. Wokeism, which had been forming slowly for decades before venturing into full public view in the 2010s, was poised to be that something. By the time the emergency was finally declared over—more than three years later—global society looked very different. Woke retributive justice and racial discrimination commanded urban life, college campuses, government agencies, and corporate boardrooms. Violent antisemitism was widespread while anti-Christian forces were stronger and bolder than ever. Transgenderism mushroomed, particularly among the young who demanded "compassion" from their elders so that they could be sterilized and mutilated. Good parenting required indulging the worst childish impulses. Equal justice and the rule of law evaporated in favor of disparate treatment. Terrorists, their apologists, and their benefactors became heroes in the struggle for liberation and equity. Censorship emerged as a critical tool protecting the weak-minded from facts or opinions that might lead them astray. The ends justified the means.

These moral inversions—and more like them—are signs of ascendant Wokeism. Their incompatibility with basic Biblical ethics is a feature of that ascendance, not a bug. Wokeism emphatically rejects Biblical morality in favor of utopian socialism. Alter the source and roots of morality and you alter morality itself. In a Woke world, there is no room for Judaism or Christianity. Nor is there room for denominational variants of Islam, Hinduism, Buddhism, or any other traditional faith compatible with the spirit of America's founding. On current trends, ascendant Wokeism and ascendant Islamism, both backed and bankrolled by an ascendant Chinese Communist Party, will terminate what remains of Western civilization before turning their fire on each other.

It is thus imperative upon those of us who care about the future of America, the future of the West, the future of the God of the Bible, the future of freedom, and future of all mature, peaceful, traditional faiths to alter those trends. It's far beyond time to fight back effectively and on multiple fronts.

As with other young or universal faiths, Wokeism isn't content with governing the lives of its adherents. It prefers to flex its muscles, enshrine its moral code as law, and impose it broadly. That's what it would mean for Wokeism to become the established religion of the United States. The legal challenges are thus well defined.

Far harder to define is the spiritual way forward. To prevail, we must reconnect with the spirit of America's founding. That reference to a founding spirit—in a discussion of religion in an inquiry into a spiritual crisis—is intentional. Notwithstanding the conventional wisdom, the founding of the American nation was a profoundly spiritual event.

Understanding the conflict between Wokeism and Americanism thus comes down to a three-pronged argument: One, we are mired in a deep spiritual crisis. Two, Wokeism is a new religion, attuned to our times, that has arisen to meet the spiritual need of the most spirit-starved Americans. Three, only a revival of America's founding spirit can preserve the American nation and the American republic.

No one said it was going to be easy.

II. THE ASCENDANCE OF WOKEISM

7. Rise of a New Faith

It's been a while since the world has brought forth a wholly new major faith. If history is any guide, young faiths can prove dangerous to all they encounter—adherent and opponent alike. Because young faiths are typically pre-canonical, sectarian differences loom large among the most zealous adherents. Tensions with opponents can be massive, particularly when the new faith derives from ethical foundations radically different from the existing faiths that surround it.

The faith we're discussing is so young that even its name is contingent. For the purposes of this inquiry I've adopted "Wokeism," but I fully expect events to soon supplant it with a more durable label.

Welcome to the 2020s and the emergence of Wokeism—a brilliant and dangerous response to the denialism of America's spiritually starved elite. Wokeism fills gaps in their lives using language and metaphor to which they can relate—allowing them to meet unarticulated needs without ever forcing them to concede the existence of those needs. Wokeism rests upon a utopian framework far different from America's own Biblical roots. The tension is inherent, palpable, and unlikely to dissipate soon.

To make matters worse, though America's spiritual crisis leveled the playing field between the two competing moral codes of biblically based Americanism and anti-biblical utopian Wokeism, American law handed the utopian code an unfair advantage. The ancient traditions and ideas necessary to complete the American civic religion are widely and correctly recognized as religious. The newfound ideas emerging to complete the utopian code are widely and mistakenly viewed as secular. In the legal constructs delineating the rules of the American public square, secular viewpoints, symbols, and celebrations are welcome; their religious counterparts are not.

Constitutional law prohibits the establishment of an official religion. It is silent on the establishment of an official ideology. It provides no clarity, however, on where one begins and the other ends. Woke utopians have seized upon that legal advantage. They don't call their constellation of metaphysical beliefs a religion. They deny emphatically that their clearly metaphysical beliefs are metaphysical. Yet the system they are crafting is just as all-encompassing as was every one of the world's majority faiths (at least until the European Counterreformation ended in a stalemate and allowed Christianity to veer in a different direction). Their Woke system espouses clear and distinctive views of economics, commerce, sexuality, community, behavior, and belief. It produces heroes, villains, martyrs, shrines, chants, holidays, and rituals. It polices blasphemy and dictates righteousness of thought. It grounds its sense of justice in sources it deems True. It has well-defined views of repentance, redemption, humanity's role in the universe, and the end of times. It has embraced rituals and religious garb. Though nearly all adherents will deny it, many of its most controversial and unique assertions make far more sense in the spiritual realm than they do in the realm of objectively observable reality. To suggest that such a comprehensive system is anything other than a religion is to demonstrate ignorance of the nature of religion.

Into the vacuum of America's spiritual crisis entered the world's first religion born of abundance, a pre-canonical faith still trying to understand itself and its place in the world. Its emergence and growth represent a deadly challenge to all faiths that preceded it—not only the comprehensive traditions it seeks to supplant, but also the American spiritual platform that looked to those faiths for completion beyond core ethics.

Like all faiths, Wokeism expresses itself in the language of its earliest times. Judaism, Christianity, Islam, Hinduism, and Buddhism emerged among populations of illiterate farmers, shepherds, nomads, merchants, and seafarers who knew little of modern science. The lines dividing the unknown from the unknowable were thin. Even assuming (as do the faithful) that one or more of these traditions represents absolute, objective, God-given Truth, the people blessed with direct revelation needed language, metaphors, and stories to communicate it to their peers—not to mention to transmit it through the generations. Their foundational stories, emphases, and rituals thus emerged among people whose realities differed greatly from those that prevail today, then evolved over time to accommodate environments equally different from our own.

Wokeism carries no such baggage. Wokeism is entirely free to craft its message in modern language and metaphor. For Wokeism to flourish, it cannot speak in old-world peasant language. It cannot vest control of its rituals in a priesthood. It cannot ground itself in gods or spirits, fate or karma, the inaccessible or the unknown. Wokeism can—must—appeal to the modern elitist mind: Urban, affluent, credentialed, professional, and mired in abundance. These people trust The Science, not God. Their authorities are credentialed experts, not priests. Their seminaries are universities, not monasteries. Their public square involves media and social media, not town centers or plazas. Perhaps most importantly, their spiritual needs range from the unarticulated to the denied.

Wokeism must thus cater to its faithful without ever conceding that it is either a faith or catering. It has done remarkably well on both counts. The Woke thinkers who found ways to meet that challenge thought deeply. They studied and tested. Wokeism is not a casual experiment. Nor is it a mere handful of political ideas and slogans. It's an all-embracing lifestyle every bit as comprehensive as Judaism, Christianity, Islam, Hinduism, and Buddhism. That much of it is still taking shape does little to alter its comprehensive nature or the threat it poses to all faith traditions that came before it.

Of direct interest to the American future, however, the comprehensive nature of Wokeism negates the American formulation. The generalized Christian ethics at the core of America's founding spirit were sufficiently universal to enable most pre-existing faiths to embrace them while relinquishing only minimal elements of their own traditions. Woke ethics, derived in many cases from a utopian perspective, are simply incompatible. Ethical Wokeism inverts many elements of America's ethical foundations.

To Americans, it's self-evident "that all men are created equal, that they are endowed by their Creator with certain unalienable rights, that among these are life, liberty and the pursuit of happiness."

To the Woke, humans are born into conditions of inherent inequality. History and society bestow upon them distinctively unequal rights, responsibilities, privileges, and expectations. While some are entitled to elevation and compensation commensurate with ancestral inequities, others are born to pay the price of that compensation in retribution for ancestral privilege. Life may be a right to those already born, but liberty is a chimera and deeply contingent. Happiness is a distraction from the cause of justice.

It hardly ends there. Woke views of biology, sex, race, gender, justice, the supernatural, the start of life, and the place of humanity within nature set the Woke apart from adherents of other faiths. Yes, the Woke may scream that theirs is not a religion, but "merely" a search for truth, a quest for justice, a desire to restructure society along the lines of equity and enlightened thinking, and a set of guidelines to conform behavior accordingly. Such denials suggest only that the American elites to whom Wokeism appeals are so divorced from the concept of a faith tradition that they no longer know what the word "religion" means. What is any religion if not a search for truth, a quest for justice, and a desire to conform both individual behavior and communal structures accordingly?

It is a testament to the founding thinkers of Wokeism that they have met this truly daunting challenge. Fulfilling the unarticulated spiritual needs of a flock committed to denial of all things spiritual is hardly easy. Few of the greatest leaders of any traditional faith have found ways to succeed. The leaders of Wokeism, unencumbered by the ballast of timelessness and free to focus exclusively on the present, have been far more successful.

Consider but a few of Wokeism's most successful forays into quasi-scientific theology:

Apocalyptic climate change is a fully eschatological vision of the end of times, in which man's sins against nature will lead the earth, the seas, and the skies to rise and smite him. Only full repentance and a radical alteration of his profligate lifestyle can bring salvation.

The trans movement is nothing less profound than the rediscovery of the soul. In a body whose genetics, reproductive physiology, and endocrinology all scream "male," what innate, unalterable, congenital element could possibly override them to declare "no, female?" Nothing observable. Nothing testable. Only a metaphysical inner essence defining a True self.

The source of continued human suffering is not "sin," but "racism." To the Woke, racism is no longer a set of attitudes or behaviors that can be overcome at the individual level. It is a pervasive, timeless curse corrupting all existing institutions and relationships. Only by inverting our natural tendencies to favor those closest to us over those further away can we even hope to defeat it.

Covid was a plague of biblical dimensions that only Woke bureaucratic experts could overcome. Many of their responses to Covid—dubious and implausible from the outset, now incontrovertibly incapable of having achieved their stated goals—became instantly ritualized. Symbolic face masks became Woke religious garb. Experimental genetic injections became rites of passage and tribal markings. Various other responses—from the songs sung to time handwashing to the ubiquitous hand sanitizer and the Lysoling of mail and groceries—manifest obvious purification rituals.

Cancel culture, social media censorship, and the mainstream media's injection of constant, repetitive editorial comment into news stories are fully familiar to anyone who has ever studied anti-blasphemy laws. Nothing running counter to the faith may be given a fair hearing, lest it cause discomfort to the faithful—or worse, cause their faith to waver. Cancellation is little more than a contemporary synonym for excommunication.

The list of Woke innovations grows with each passing year. It is entirely unsurprising that they all take hold most closely among the American enclaves most distant from traditional faith. Those whose life decisions have taken them furthest into the spiritual vacuum are those most likely to grasp for anything that can meet an unarticulated spiritual need without roiling their self-images as having moved beyond the superstitions of old.

Wokeism has much work to do as it fleshes itself out fully. It's likely to experience considerable infighting before it can fully canonize its still-shifting beliefs. It has already, however, passed the point of no return. Wokeism is a full-blown religion boasting huge numbers of adherents. Love it or hate it, embrace it or fear it, it is incumbent upon us all to treat Wokeism seriously.

8. The Eschatology of Climate Change

If Wokeism is a new religion whose many scientific-sounding arguments are mere veils shrouding metaphysics and theology, the oldest and best developed area of Woke pseudoscientific spirituality is the end-times myth of apocalyptic climate change. Why? I confess that I don't know. Many spiritual needs make sense to me as answers offered to pressing, unknowable questions. I understand why many people feel the need to comprehend the creation of the earth. I understand why many people feel the need to know where we were before birth and where we go after death. I don't know why many people feel the need to believe in apocalypse, but I observe that they do.

Eschatology—a belief about the end of days—arises in some form in many faith traditions. There are only two plausible explanations for such universality, one external, the other internal. One, there could be an underlying external Truth to the end of days that each of these traditions has attempted to access (with all faithful believing that theirs has done so most correctly). Two, there could be some deep, internal, human spiritual need that only a belief in end times can fulfill. Either way, Wokeism is hardly the exception in giving a central role to the repentance needed to save humanity from hurtling toward destruction.

Not all beliefs about a changing climate are eschatological and not all people concerned with the earth's changing climate are Woke. Wokeism simply embeds some eminently reasonable scientific inquiries and economic considerations within an eschatological framework—then seizes ownership of the entire discussion. The sleight-of-hand implication is that rational observations and concerns imply the truth of their deeply metaphysical Woke interpretation and mythology. From there, the leap from established apocalyptic concerns to draconian, authoritarian power grabs follows as a matter of course.

This approach is hardly novel. The history of philosophy is replete with rational thinkers who derived some element of their faith, then leaped immediately to particularist conclusions. René Descartes labored mightily to prove that the world could only have arisen through the actions of a sentient deity—then quickly concluded the Truth of his Catholic Church.

Blaise Pascal similarly used rudimentary game theory to prove that the utility differences between eternal heaven and eternal hell should motivate anyone who placed any non-zero probability on God's existence to adhere to a Catholic lifestyle. Needless to say, Protestants, Jews, and Muslims might have followed the logic of these Catholic thinkers until almost the very last step before concluding that something had gone awry.

Wokeism thus draws upon a longstanding tradition that has pervaded the writing—and logic—of some of history's greatest thinkers. In today's world, Woke eschatologists have woven an elegant tapestry of climate science, resource politics, and their apocalyptic vision into a single, compelling Climate Change myth.

The basic science of climate study is straightforward and non-controversial. The earth's climate has never been constant. History records cooler phases and warmer phases, each distributing costs and benefits unevenly around the globe. Past epochs of warming and cooling have moved fertile land from one area to another, raised and lowered sea levels, and altered the navigability of rivers. The causes of these changes are complex, but it seems eminently plausible that surface activity may be among them. Until recently, the climactic contributions of surface activity were negligible. In recent centuries, the human population has exploded, as has our ability to harness energy. Surface activity capable of contributing to climate change has grown correspondingly. Whether it's still minimal is unknown, but it's certainly greater today that at any point in the past.

Scientists have built many models in their attempts to understand climate. Two observations characterize all such models: They exhibit tremendous sensitivity to minor variations in input, and few if any of their predictions have proved accurate. Such models are hallmarks of poorly understood scientific phenomena. Wokeism ignores the low quality of these models while touting the existence of scientific models consistent with their eschatological beliefs.

Wokeism also exploits a dangerous distinction between scientific inquiry and "the scientific community." Scientific communities face many incentives unrelated to improving the world's understanding of science. Institutional funding and individual prestige are at least as important.

Those imperatives promote only climate scientists whose models help validate the preferred narrative of those funding their research—a group comprised almost entirely of elite, affluent, credentialed professionals riven with unmet and denied spiritual needs. For these funders and scientists, Woke eschatology does more than merely fill such a need. It puts them—personally—at the center of the drive to fix the world. It's hard to think of an unmet spiritual need more central to either the human psyche or the egos of those who see themselves as inherently superior to the surrounding masses. The incentives thus snowball. Credentialed scientists eager to promote the Woke narrative of massive, imminent, cataclysmic climate change thrive. Those presenting skeptical, nuanced, or opposing views face short, isolated, unhappy careers.

To the non-Woke who understand this incentive system, the very structure of "the scientific community" pursuing climate change raises intense skepticism—as did the highly credentialed twentieth century scientists working for tobacco companies who could find no link between smoking and cancer. Woke dominance of the elite and the credentialing factories known as universities, however, guarantee that few of the non-Woke understand the incentives shaping modern science.

The actual state of climate science thus establishes that models with minimal predictive ability, funded to predict a looming cataclysm, and exhibiting severe sensitivity to input specifications, can predict a cataclysmic outcome when given appropriate inputs. Nothing more. That's hardly enough to power an eschatological movement. Wokeism thus glides effortlessly from climate science to climate politics—and from there into climate mythology.

Those politics harken back to a debate that has raged at least since Thomas Malthus introduced the notion of resource depletion around the turn of the nineteenth century. As an important precursor to the entire utopian worldview that would soon follow, Malthus was deeply concerned that the accelerating use of resources in the early industrial age was straining the earth. He predicted that the world would soon run out of resources. His prescription was that his contemporaries curb their seemingly insatiable appetites, cease experimenting and advancing, and instead conserve the world's resources base.

Concerns about resource depletion have never left the environmental discussion, even as consumption has skyrocketed with no signs of imminent depletion. In every generation, some new hysteric arises to announce that—this time—the world really is running out of resources, suffering irreparable damage, and dooming future generations to a miserable existence. In the late twentieth century that mantle fell to famed biologist Paul Ehrlich, whose concern was so great that he predicted, in 1980, the demise of England by the year 2000. (Spoiler: England made it into the twenty-first century). In response, economist Julian Simon bet him that the long-term trend of free market commodity prices was downward—a result incompatible with increasing shortages. The two agreed on a fixed basket of commodities and a fixed ten-year term. In 1990, Simon won easily; every commodity in the basket had declined in price.

Old habits die hard. The timeless beauty of resource depletion for those who believe in it is that it always justifies draconian reforms. Surely, no one could believe that their personal short-term comfort is more important than the future of life on earth! For those seeking to transform their societies, the fear of such a cataclysm provides a plausible justification for insisting upon massive, widespread behavioral change. More importantly, it justifies the draconian centralization of authority necessary to impose such behavioral change on an unwilling population. Climate politics thus follows a venerable and predictable pattern that is completely untethered to climate science; it is, quite simply, political.

The blurring of the scientific and the political abounds throughout the Woke literature. Klaus Schwab, head of the elite, Woke World Economic Forum, provides a masterful example of the genre. His *Great Reset/Great Narrative* series prescribing the global future of a post-Covid world rests upon two strong-form assumptions: One, we're heading towards a truly apocalyptic climate crisis. Two, the governmental actions taken to combat Covid exemplify laudatory collective action in the service of the common good. In Schwab's Woke framing, these two assertions are self-evident truths that only fringe "deniers" would even bother to challenge.

Reading a bit more carefully than Schwab might like reveals that his assertions are far from matters of consensus. Yes, most people likely accept that the earth's climate is in one of its periodic warming phases and recognize that the global spread of Covid from Wuhan, China in early 2020 posed a genuine public health challenge. Nearly everyone but the most devout Woke, however, would balk at Schwab's final leap of logic—much as non-Catholics would have told Descartes and Pascal: "This far but no farther." For Schwab's narrative to work, climate change must be apocalyptic rather than merely concerning; governmental anti-Covid actions must have been models of excellence rather than plausible-if-misguided steps taken amidst conditions of hysteria, uncertainty, and anxiety (if not outright disasters).

In other words, Schwab's fringe "deniers" are hardly fringe. They define almost the entire political right and most of the non-elite, non-Woke left. Yet it's only fidelity to the strongest form of Schwab's two arguments that can possibly underpin his radical plan for the future. That plan in a nutshell? Authoritarian global enforcement, of the sort we experienced with Covid, to address the imminent, truly cataclysmic, climate meltdown.

Miraculously, along the way, the wise men and women charged with implementing Schwab's global solution will also enhance welfare, promote income equality, and preserve important human freedoms. How or why any of these second-tier concerns should emerge enhanced is far from clear, but the wisdom and benevolence of the new leadership class will attend to them ably.

Schwab's conclusions fail dismally as matters of logic, science, and empiricism. For the Woke, however, they provide a deeply comforting spiritual message that speaks to a human need so deep and so clear that many faith traditions preach something similar: Repent, follow the precepts of the true faith, and the world itself will breathe a sigh of relief. All will become right. A new era will dawn. Justice will prevail. Pretty standard end-of-days stuff.

Woke eschatology combines suspect science and authoritarian politics into a dark vision: Humanity is living out of harmony with nature. As people revel in their orgiastic consumption of energy, mother earth—Gaia—weeps. Her resources, her children, the very elements that make Gaia Gaia are disappearing. Callous, thoughtless mankind bleeds her dry, sapping her essence to fulfill its insatiable, base desires. Gaia screams in pain. The rage builds within her. Benevolent goddess that she is, Gaia sends warnings. She warms herself slowly, begging humanity to repent. "Change your ways!" she implores. "Cease your exploitation. If you must consume energy, draw it from resources I can renew. Turn back from your crimes against me, your crimes against your planet, your crimes against nature! For if you do not, the earth will tremble, the skies will cloud, and the seas will rise to smite you!" Is it any wonder that the very messianic and very Woke Barack Obama described his nomination for the Presidency as "the moment when the rise of the oceans began to slow and our planet began to heal?"

In today's world, proper scientific inquiries into the nature and workings of the earth's climate are critical. Political and economic concerns about the effects of warming or cooling, natural disasters, changes to sea level, movements of arable land, and related phenomena are worthy topics for policy debate. Apocalyptic Climate Change, on the other hand, makes sense only in a deeply spiritual realm. The Woke aversion to spiritual terms like apocalypse, eschatology, or end times do little to alter that reality. Apocalyptic Climate Change allows Wokeism to feed a deep, critical, unarticulated need of today's elite without conceding the existence of spirit. It is Wokeism's most complete and masterful coup to date.

9. The Woke Soul

Climate change eschatology is the lowest hanging fruit in the new religion of Wokeism. The parallels between climate change and the more traditional tales of Armageddon are hard to miss. Most of the other unmet spiritual needs that Wokeism addresses are subtler. Consider the sort of basic metaphysical questions we've all likely asked ourselves. What makes me *me*? Where were my children before I met their other parent? Why do I feel a sense of loss when loved ones die—even though I can still see their lifeless bodies? These questions are deep. They're difficult. They have no answers within the physical realm. They belong to the realm of the unknowable, the metaphysical, the spiritual.

Traditional faiths—all traditional faiths—provide answers to such questions. The mechanism they use to answer them is a metaphysical concept called the soul. Specific conceptions of the soul may differ, but all faiths recognize the existence of a timeless spirit that inhabits the body. All faiths recognize that people combine an intangible essence with a physical shell—and furthermore, that it is the inner essence that defines the true self.

What, however, can be said of the spiritually starved elite at the heart of America's spiritual crisis? Don't they ask themselves the same penetrating questions? Don't they need answers as badly as do those of faith? Doesn't their rejection of spirituality and metaphysics deprive them of those answers?

It's hard to think of a better example of an unarticulated spiritual need. America's scientifically-oriented, credentialed, professional elite must find some way to generate answers without conceding that they have left the empirical realms of observable, testable science—realms that very clearly cannot provide answers to these very important questions. That's where Wokeism comes to the rescue: With a theory and a movement that speaks the language of science, keeps the actual answer cloaked, yet serves precisely the role that every traditional faith assigned to the soul.

This deep dive into the metaphysics of Wokeism—the areas that the Woke like to pretend are scientific despite clear evidence to the contrary—

is likely to be uncomfortable for all, Woke and anti-Woke alike. Nevertheless—or perhaps because of that discomfort—it is critical.

It's not hard to see that, protestations to the contrary, Wokeism has a metaphysics. Science is a process of inquiry about observable, testable phenomena. If something can be neither observed nor tested, science can have nothing to say about it. That's not to say that such phenomena are unreal. In fact, many essential, defining beliefs of every traditional faith system are neither observable nor testable. The faithful nevertheless believe deeply in their Truth, and it is far above my paygrade to determine who among them may be wrong. The same is true for Wokeism.

The Woke very clearly do believe in the soul. Though they will deny it and decry it, they cannot disprove it: The deeply controversial Trans Movement is nothing less profound than the Woke rediscovery of the soul.

The metaphysics of transgenderism are central to the battle pitting the American Spirit against the Great Awokening because they have assumed center stage in the culture wars. Gender issues today are central to nearly every discussion about education, public accommodation, health care, manners, and even the evolution of the English language. Discussions and debates incapable of seeing the Trans Movement for what it is cannot provide either its adherents or its opponents with the respect their arguments deserve.

As with many excursions into Woke thought, it's important to start with clear definitions—never easy given the Woke penchant for deconstruction. For present purposes:

"Transwomen" are people born genetically and biologically male who declare publicly that their gender is female.

"Transmen" are people born genetically and biologically female who declare publicly that their gender is male.

"Transes" is a plural term I've coined because there doesn't seem to be any generally acceptable term for "transmen and transwomen" (the term "trannies" is now considered a pejorative).

The "Trans Movement" is comprised of all people who believe that gender declarations, rather than biology, define truth. It is obviously far larger than the group of people who consider themselves transes.

This Trans Movement entered broad public consciousness less than a decade ago with a fight over bathroom signage laws in North Carolina. Today it is unquestionably a mass movement to which millions of Americans belong. As such, it warrants serious consideration and treatment. What is it?

It's not a rights movement. Rights movements—like the Civil Rights Movement of the 1950s and 1960s—seek equal treatment, in law and in fact, for groups recognized as distinct. They don't seek to obliterate distinctions. Martin Luther King, Jr. didn't march asserting that he was a white man. He didn't ask anyone to acknowledge his whiteness or to ignore racial distinctiveness. He marched as a proud black man shouting the illegitimacy of all laws that afforded him a legal status different from that handed a similarly situated white man.

A rights movement focused on transes would accept that transwomen and women are distinct. It would focus on the challenges transes face in navigating life and in gaining full acceptance. One faction might argue that any law that distinguishes men from women must group people as they declare themselves to be rather than as they were born. A more moderate faction might accept that there are indeed environments in which the presence of transwomen might cause women so much agony (e.g., shelters for battered women) that differential treatment might be warranted. Still other factions might believe that the appropriate categorization is not the mere declaration of gender but rather some specific concrete (and perhaps irreversible) step taken towards living in line with that declaration.

No such factions are permitted in today's Trans Movement. The movement's mantra, "transwomen are women," reflects its central belief that biology is not destiny. Doctors or parents who preserve the timeless practice of declaring a newborn "boy" or "girl" are reactionary hatemongers, consigning innocent babes to a potentially debilitating lifetime of societally induced stereotyping.

Today's Trans Movement is a radical departure from the parts of the gay rights movement focused on the accommodation of transes as it existed as recently as a decade ago. Rights-based positions that were long viewed as profoundly open to transes, deeply compassionate, and highly progressive are today deemed hurtful and hateful.

In contemplating the metaphysical nature of the Trans Movement, it's important to appreciate how and why metaphysics is more important than mundane arguments about rights and equality. It's hard to miss the two most glaring casualties that the Trans Movement has trampled: gay rights and women's rights.

Far from being an outgrowth of the rights-based movements seeking equality for women or for homosexuals, today's Trans Movement runs roughshod over those groups. In the Woke hierarchy of intersectional oppression, "ciswomen" (i.e., heterosexual genetic females) and homosexuals are less oppressed than transes. Like all lesser oppressed groups, they must subordinate their own claims and rights to the needs of those suffering greater oppression. Anyone advocating different priorities is, by definition, an oppressor—and thus an enemy of the Woke. As a result—and notwithstanding its insistence to the contrary—the Trans Movement has become a hotbed of misogyny and homophobia.

The debilitating effects of inserting transwomen—always with male genetics, usually with male musculature, often with male personalities, and sometimes with male genitalia—into women's sports and previously women-only safe spaces has been reported widely. The consequences of these incursions have been precisely as any advocate for women's welfare would have predicted: Sexual assaults in high schools, rapes in women's prisons, discomfort in women's shelters, and male dominance of women's sports are among the most obvious.

Women who note these problems—including more than a few feminists with previously-impeccable Woke credentials—are immediately deemed TERFs (trans-exclusionary radical feminists); J.K. Rowling is likely the most prominent example. Wokeism casts all TERFs out of the faith, dooming them to wander in the wilderness rubbing shoulders with deplorables, conservatives, traditionalists, and other undesirables. The Woke treatment of TERFs—many of whom advocate strongly for education and public accommodation policies designed to ease life and acceptance for transes—is perhaps the clearest demonstration that today's Trans Movement is not a rights movement.

On the homophobic front, a growing number of gay Americans are awakening to what has happened to their own hugely successful rights movement—and worse, to their reputation. Some are coming to recognize the rush to transition children and teens upon the earliest deviation from stereotypical gender roles as a form of gay conversion therapy: Rather than allowing these children to mature into healthy bodies as gay (or straight) adults, the Trans Movement advocates mutilating their bodies and overriding their hormones.

Other members of the gay community, having spent decades securing acceptance as stable families and contributors to the healthy fabric of American communal life, are still in shock over the transformation of the organizations that once argued for their own equal rights into groups committed to sexualizing and mutilating children—and to undermining the sanctity of the family. Their shock is understandable. Activist groups founded with a firm grounding in the principles of equal protection, civil rights, and the rule of law have become religious organizations promoting Wokeism.

To date, however, relatively few gay leaders have been brave enough to step forward to draw a clear line between supporting stable gay families and opposing the oversexualization and mutilation of children. The current posture of "LGBTQIA+ advocacy" (Lesbian, Gay, Bisexual, Transgender, Queer, Intersex, Asexual, and more) is giving gay Americans a bad name—at precisely the moment that gay men and lesbians had finally gained broad societal acceptance.

That transformation of gay rights activism in America was so abrupt, so jarring, and so perfectly timed that some contend that it was merely a cynical ploy driven by money, media, and politics. Activism is a business and professional activists want to stay in business. In 2015, the lobby for gay rights committed the cardinal sin of professional activism: It won a decisive victory. In less than fifty years it had moved gay men and lesbians from despised, openly mistreated minorities living largely in the shadows to marriageable members of the societal mainstream. That's phenomenally successful activism. So successful, in fact, that it threatened to put the professional activists out of business. When the Supreme Court declared gay marriage the law of the land in *Obergefell*, gay rights activism slid from the forefront of America's expanding constellation of rights into a sideline, policing pockets of anti-gay activity, discrimination, and violence. Its big battles were over. No one reasonably believes that homosexuality is a barrier to a full, open, honest life, career, or family in today's America.

Cynics can thus easily point to a lobby that manufactured a cause—mere months after scoring a total victory in its previous battle—for the sole purpose of perpetuating its own relevance. The North Carolina bathroom battles erupted before the ink was even dry on *Obergefell*. To drive the case home even further, a handful of prominent billionaires are indeed bankrolling the medical establishment's enshrinement of sexual reassignment surgery as an "affirmation" rather than as the denial it obviously is.

Such cynical arguments aren't wrong, but they're too narrow. They miss the big picture. Even the best funded campaigns can't sell a mass market product that no one wants to buy. It doesn't matter how badly gay rights activists needed a new issue. It doesn't matter how much money they spent. If they couldn't craft a message that spoke deeply to the members of their target market, they'd never close the deal. Yet close the deal they did. That's a success worth pondering. To flourish, the Trans Movement's message had to touch tens of millions of Americans, most of whom had not previously given the issue a moment's thought, and few of whom had ever knowingly met a trans. That's a tall order. Yet it succeeded. How? Why?

Such questions deserve answers. Before we can answer them, however, we must eliminate one other potential characterization of the Trans Movement: The Woke are adamant that it has nothing to do with mental illness.

Unlike the concept of a rights-based organization—a mischaracterization that many members of the Trans Movement embrace—the notion that transes may be suffering from an abnormal mental or physical condition is held exclusively by opponents of the Trans Movement. To the Woke, even suggesting such a possibility qualifies as hate speech. In fact, it's such a transgression that it is *always* wrong. Within the Trans Movement, not only are some or most people who declare a gender misaligned with their biology correct, *all* such people are correct. No mentally ill person, whatever their other problems may be, would make such a claim.

Yet denial, no matter how vociferous and sincere, is insufficient to make a characterization inaccurate. After all, gender dysphoria is a condition in which a person's psychological and emotional states send messages at odds with genetics and biology. Such a misalignment must be so painful and disruptive that it's almost impossible for non-sufferers to comprehend. Fortunately, we live in a world of scientific marvels in which surgery, lifelong medication, and counseling can combine to let the afflicted lead fulfilling, productive lives.

By what logic, however, are transes the first and only mentally and physically healthy people whose brains cannot perceive objective reality and whose bodies require radical surgery and a lengthy, complicated medical regimen?

The answers cannot rest upon a mere redefinition of terms. No one— inside or outside the Trans Movement—disputes certain factual observations. Nearly all humans are born with sex chromosomes that are either XX or XY. Nearly all of those born XX develop reproductive physiology and endocrinology consistent with being a healthy female. Nearly all of those born XY develop reproductive physiology and endocrinology consistent with being a healthy male. While the Trans Movement does include concern for the tiny number of exceptions, its primary focus remains on those whose genetics and biology conform to one of these two basic patterns—yet whose internal states express as something other than 100% female (for those born XX) or 100% male (for those born XY).

There can be only two possible answers as to how an internal mechanism (i.e., a human brain) reading genetically and biologically consistent XX signals could conclude that it is something other than 100% female: Either that brain is mistaken or it is also reading additional signals sending divergent messages. If the brain is making a mistake (i.e., misreading consistent signals), it should seem to qualify as a mental illness—a logical possibility that the Woke reject out of hand. The only remaining conclusion is thus that something must be sending the brain a conflicting message. The healthy trans brain thus processes multiple messages to arrive at a gender identity that is subtler, more perceptive, and more accurate than the blunt polarity of the 100% male / 100% female gender binary.

Fair enough. But that conclusion merely replaces one set of questions with another. It's one thing to posit the existence of a source sending signals that differ from those of genetics and biology. It's another to identify that source. If there is indeed something real, internal to the individual, sending signals that are at least as valid as those emerging from that same individual's genetics, physiology, and endocrinology, what is it?

It's certainly neither observable nor testable—meaning that it's not a scientific phenomenon. If it were, the obvious first step in treating those expressing discomfort with their biological gender would be to run some tests. Do they manifest the observable source of genuine transgenderism? Or are they merely exhibiting symptoms deriving from some other cause? No one would ever recommend treatment of any sort prior to running such tests.

Such testing is not part of the Woke approach to transes precisely because the source of the overriding gender signal is neither observable nor testable. It exists outside the physical world. Where might it be?

Could it lie within the experiential realm and thus be psychological in nature? Not according to the Woke. In fact, a reliance on an individual's experiences would undermine the entire movement. If a transwoman is merely a genetic male whose experiences to date send a psychological female signal, perhaps some additional experiences might alter that signal? Such a possibility seems particularly acute when applied to children whose experiential bases are shallow and whose psychological responses are still in formation. It would also render meaningless the idea that people are born with a gender identity. Experiential explanations make eminent sense if gender is acquired and malleable. They are nonsensical if gender is innate and fixed—a core Woke belief.

Furthermore, even in adults, were the counter-genetic signals rooted in the psychological processing of experiential data, the front-line treatment would almost certainly involve deep therapy and reprogramming—precisely the opposite of the indulgence, "affirmation," medication, and surgery the Trans Movement advocates. No, the central claim of the entire Trans Movement is that the counter-genetic signal provides the only accurate defining recognition of the individual's true gender identity. "A transwoman is a woman!" is a stark declaration that in an individual whose genetics scream "male" but whose internal messaging shouts "female," the internal voice speaks Truth while the genetic externalities present falsehoods. Identifying the source of that true internal signal would thus seem to be of tantamount importance. Having ruled out the realms of the physical and the experiential, what potential sources remain?

The Woke themselves offer few insights. Why? Perhaps because the only plausible answer makes them uncomfortable—and the Woke are hardly known for welcoming their own discomfort. Comfortable or not, however, such core questions underpinning such an important contemporary movement deserve answers. As with all things that seem to make little sense—yet are indeed occurring—the answers must lie where few have been willing to look. Where might that be?

The immense appeal of the Trans Movement provides a clue. A movement that touches so few lives, yet has such broad resonance, must speak to people at a visceral level. It must address a widespread need— albeit one that is rarely articulated and often denied. What unarticulated need might the notion of an internal source of true identity address for the many Woke who are not trans themselves and who may not even know any transes personally?

The answer lies in the spiritual realm. The Trans Movement fills one of the most basic spiritual vacuums created when America's elite rejected traditional faith. Listen closely, and you can even hear a tale that is both meaningful and beautiful:

We humans arrive in this world with two selves. Our outer selves are physical and tangible, genetic, biological, and sexed. Our inner selves are intangible, psychological, emotional, and gendered. Our outer selves are little more than shells within which our true inner selves must function. Only our inner selves define our true essence. Only the inner self makes us who we are. Only the inner self gives meaning to life. Our task, as individuals, is to align our lives with our essential inner truths.

The majority among us—those of us fortunate enough to have been born with perfectly aligned inner and outer selves—should be grateful for the gift. Those who must alter their outer selves to align their bodies with essential inner truth face a far greater challenge. The Woke believe that a just society must eliminate all hurdles impeding that alignment. A just society must take all steps necessary to ease all transitions from falsehood to truth.

That beautiful story is hardly radical. Every faith tradition tells a similar tale. It's critical to explaining our uniqueness as a species and our further uniqueness as individuals. Every faith tradition embraces—as a central tenet—the idea that we're more than our bodies.

Wokeism shares the traditional belief that only our incorporeal elements are capable of greatness, elevation, or enlightenment. Our physical bodies trap us in the mundane realm. Only transcendence of physicality allows us to access the spiritual or the divine. Only our transcendent elements can know the beauty of love, of friendship, of connection, of belonging. Such metaphysical beliefs are hardly novel. Numerous faiths derived them long before Wokeism gave them its uniquely contemporary twist.

The Trans Movement represents nothing short of the Woke rediscovery of the soul. It provides a story and a belief system capable of elevating the Woke beyond the mundane, physical, material existence many have chosen for themselves. Even better, it does so without resorting to the ancient languages and pastoral metaphors that the Woke disdain. It rests entirely in the legalistic language of rights, the political language of exploitation, and the scientific language of surgery and medicine. In a masterstroke, the Trans Movement provides silent, secret soulcraft to those who could never admit to the existence of the soul or the need for soulfulness.

The Woke rediscovery of the soul also provides a coherent justification for full-term abortion on demand. There's no reason the Woke should feel bound by the Vatican's declaration that "ensoulment" happens almost immediately after conception. Perhaps the gendered Woke soul arrives only at the moment of live birth. If so, a gestating fetus—at any stage—really is just a clump of cells. The tension between a woman's right to personal medical choices and the fetal right to life fades away even in the latest stage of pregnancy. All that an abortion does is eliminate an unfilled outer shell; the true inner essence that would soon define humanity has never come into play.

Admission of the truth about the Trans Movement thus clarifies that nearly all Woke political positions and policy preferences pertaining to life, birth, childhood, parenting, and family, are religious beliefs. That's hardly a radical proposition. Nearly all non-Woke political positions and policy preferences pertaining to life, birth, childhood, parenting, and family, are also religious beliefs. Such issues are inherently metaphysical or spiritual. Questions like: When does life begin? Or what defines the true self? do not lend themselves to empirical inquiry, observation, or replicable experimentation. Only faith can provide meaningful answers.

Wokeism, however, can concede neither that truth nor its centrality to the faith because doing so would disturb a flock fiercely proud of its antagonism to religion. As a result—and again like some members of traditional religions asked to justify their beliefs using only science or logic—the Woke typically resort to slandering anyone who even dares to ask these most obvious of questions. Nevertheless, proper identification of Woke arguments and policy preferences is critical to informing both debate and resolution.

That criticality ties our revelation of the Trans Movement as the Woke rediscovery of the soul back to a major theme. Wokeism is an ingenious response to the deep but unarticulated spiritual needs of America's fiercely anti-religious young, urban, affluent, credentialed, professional elite. Wokeism addresses those needs while keeping its spiritual dimension cloaked. Not every Woke idea catches fire, however. Those that do are those most attuned to an unmet need. When Wokeism ventures into territory that appears perplexing to outsiders while generating widespread intense passion among the Woke, the message is there for all who are willing to see: It is filling a gaping chasm in the lives of its adherents.

The Trans Movement exploded into public consciousness because it filled a spiritual vacuum with an elegant tale spun entirely in the language that those most in need could hear. As Woke soulcraft, the Trans Movement may provide the clearest demonstration to date of the central role that Wokeism plays as a proposed solution to America's spiritual crisis.

10. Woke Racism

When it comes to assessing inherent human spiritual needs, it's hard to imagine any concept more important than evil. Every human who has ever lived, in any human society that has ever existed, at any point in history, has noticed that bad things happen to good people, and vice-versa. Why? Is there truly no justice in the universe? If not, is there any point in being good or virtuous? Is society even possible?

As disturbing as it might be to think that evil is more important than good, it would be foolhardy to pretend that it isn't. It's both easy and common for people to take good things for granted. It's even easier among those blessed to live in abundance, for whom basic necessities are rarely if ever threatened. It's far tougher to let go of injustice or unfairness. It's impossible to miss that the decent and worthy often suffer while the cruel and violent prevail, that death strikes callously, that disasters arrive indiscriminately. These occurrences have all brought deep and abiding pain—and confusion—to every person who has ever lived. America's spiritually starved elite are no exception.

The need to grapple with evil and injustice is so deeply ingrained in the human psyche that even the utopians, Marxists, and critical theorists retained it. Though their writings dispensed with God, ethics, and goodness, they had little choice but to retain evil. In their frameworks, evil persists as a consequence of an unjust, exploitation-based status quo. The leveling and transcendence of that status quo will, of necessity, usher humanity into the utopian era.

Of course, these anti-spiritualists could hardly admit that they were preserving this quintessentially spiritual concept. They had to cloak it in social, economic, or political terms. For Marx, "the bourgeoise," or capitalists, were always to blame. Were it not for their rapacious exploitation of labor, justice would have prevailed long ago! Critical Theory made it even easier. If all of history is a struggle between oppressors and the oppressed, the source of evil is self-evident: Oppression! Who were the oppressors? Easier still: Anyone who ever emerged victorious from a struggle and got to impose a solution.

In contemporary Wokeism, the sociological term that has replaced "evil" is "racism." "Racism" in the Woke lexicon is very different from "racism" in standard pre-Woke English. Until quite recently, everyone understood "racism" as the belief that innate racial differences divide humanity into distinct categories, that different rules, standards, expectations, and responsibilities apply to each category, that judgment of an individual is contingent upon the group to which he belongs, and that the actions of an individual reflect upon his group. In other words, racism was a set of attitudes, often enshrined in law and practice, that could be overcome.

That's not what Wokeism means when it calls someone or something "racist." One of the most potent weapons in the woke arsenal is "deconstruction," the severing of a word from its long-understood meaning and the subsequent assignment of a new meaning more congenial to the needs of the Woke. The deconstruction and redefinition of "racism" and "racist" is among Wokeism's most stunning successes.

The very elite, proudly Woke Aspen Institute provided a wonderful redefinition: Structural racism is "a system in which public policies, institutional practices, cultural representations, and other norms work in various, often reinforcing ways to perpetuate racial group inequity. It identifies dimensions of our history and culture that have allowed privileges associated with 'whiteness' and disadvantages associated with 'color' to endure and adapt over time...Structural racism is not something that a few people or institutions choose to practice. Instead, it has been a feature of the social, economic, and political systems in which we all exist."

Note the critical adjective: Structural. Aspen, true to its elite scholarly roots, understood that the phenomenon it was describing was not actually "racism," but rather "structural racism." The concept overlays structural inequality with racial group identity. Wokeism puts the two together to argue that history has been irredeemably racist. Because history has been structurally racist, anyone who seeks to preserve any element of tradition is necessarily working to preserve a racist structure—and is thus inherently racist. With this marvel of deconstruction, progressivism gives itself the right to slander as racist anyone who speaks favorably about any element of the status quo.

In recent years the preferred adjective has evolved from structural to systemic, but the concept has remained untouched. In colloquial Woke discourse, the scholarly adjective is often dropped. Racism now wafts through the ether to define the social, economic, and political systems in which we all must operate. Racism is baked into existence, independent of the attitudes, utterances, or behavior of any individual, institution, organization, corporation, or government. In the presence of such racist structures, the mere acts of existing or attempting to muddle through life are racist and provocative. Actual racism, when it arises, serves mostly to muddy the water.

Racism plays the role in Wokeism that evil does in traditional faiths. The Woke preach an intense, burning hatred of racism. What the Woke call "antiracism" is a central element of the Woke identity. That Woke antiracism requires racial categorization, disparate treatment, group rather than individual identity, and a focus on immutable characteristics is irrelevant. It's impolite to notice that leading Woke theorists of antiracism preach explicit racial discrimination. It's hateful to highlight that Woke antiracism is a blinding, explicit, textbook example of a racist ideology— as racism was universally understood prior to the Woke deconstruction. It's beyond the pale to explain that racism, which was once a very respectable ideology, is reviled today precisely because of the ideological properties that Woke antiracism has embraced.

At least, such is true in Woke circles, where "racism" is jargon for the initiates and intentionally misleading to ensnare the well-intentioned uninitiated. To the Woke, "racism" has truly Manichean properties. All Woke beliefs, assertions, propositions, and actions are antiracist even when they are blindingly racist. All anti-Woke beliefs, assertions, propositions, and actions are racist even when they have nothing to do with race—and explicitly racist when they challenge or subvert the racial categorizations at the heart of true racism. Colorblindness is perhaps the clearest example of an antidote to actual racism that racist Woke antiracists view as supportive of a systemically racist status quo, and therefore racist. (Bonus points for readers who followed that last sentence).

The centrality of "racism" to the Woke worldview, however, runs far deeper. Like most all-encompassing core theological concepts, it can be hard for the uninitiated to grasp. The Woke insistence that its discussions are sociological rather than spiritual makes it even harder.

At one extreme, Woke "racism" overlaps with the way that speakers of American English understand the term. Dylann Roof, for example, was a white supremacist who shot up a Black church in Charleston, SC, in June 2015. Everyone in America recognized that he was a racist and spoke out forcefully against him. Roof found almost no support from anyone other than his fellows in the tiny fringe white supremacist movement. Woke and non-Woke were in complete agreement that he and his actions were both racist and evil.

But Wokeism expands the notion to unrecognizable extremes. Thanks to the brilliance of intersectionality, "racism" has become an umbrella term subsuming xenophobia, sexism, misogyny, homophobia, Islamophobia, transphobia, and any other insults that seem to fit the mood of the moment (though not, it is important to note, antisemitism). Because all critical-theoretic struggles are merely manifestations of the same struggle, the Woke can deride any member of any "traditional oppressor" class as racist independent of specifics.

Furthermore—and here's where things get really interesting—all that is necessary for the Woke to find racism in an event is that it evoke some real or imagined form of exploitation. Thus, to pick the most obvious example, every police shooting of a black suspect is racist. It's unnecessary to show that race played any role in any specific shooting. Nor is it even imperative that the cop be white. All police shootings of black suspects evoke an era in which white authority figures brutalized black people with impunity. Thus, notwithstanding the attention paid to George Floyd's death, almost none of it focused on determining whether or not race played any role in the specific incident of the day.

In a similar vein, in any dispute between a man and a woman, the factual support for their respective positions is irrelevant. Anyone agreeing with the male's perspective is necessarily evoking a historic patriarchy in which women and their opinions were devalued (if not disregarded altogether).

To the Woke, it doesn't much matter whether the evocations represent genuine historical eras, occasional worst-case abuses, or even fabricated Hollywood depictions. What matters is that the emotions they stir are real and present—or perhaps more pointedly, that the emotions that Woke activists and media personalities can stir in others are real and present. Thus, the mere fact that many people seem willing to believe that rich prep school kids routinely engage in debauched bacchanalia replete with rape gangs should have been enough to deny Brett Kavanaugh a seat on the Supreme Court. Forget his personal behavior or his legal qualifications. His mere continued presence as a public figure "forces" the Woke, many of whom see themselves as past or potential victims of sexual improprieties, to think about spoiled, self-entitled, gang-raping rich preppies.

As a technical matter, of course, exploitative and inappropriate male/female conflicts favoring the male are properly labeled either sexist or misogynist, not racist. Because intersectionality binds together all struggles as mere manifestations of a single struggle, however, the Woke rarely need to be quite that technical. For the most part, only the most professional outlets—like the Aspen Institute—even feign such precision. During the 2016 election, for example, the Huffington Post performed valiantly. It appended a disclaimer to every article mentioning the GOP's candidate: "Editor's note: Donald Trump regularly incites political violence and is a serial liar, rampant xenophobe, racist, misogynist, and birther who has repeatedly pledged to ban all Muslims — 1.6 billion members of an entire religion — from entering the U.S." Even that seemed like too much work once Trump became President. The publication simply adopted the far more common practice of sprinkling Woke pejoratives liberally into the body of its articles. Besides, that 2016 disclaimer is already dated. Anything more recent would certainly have added "transphobic" to the list. Far easier to stick with the hardy perennial of racism.

Moreover, to the Woke, racism is not merely the relabeling of "evil" in terms lacking theological connotations. It is also the original sin that gave birth to America. The Woke 1619 Project dismisses 1776 as the founding date of America. In its telling, the 1619 arrival of a slave ship birthed an America indelibly tainted with racism. That assertion may be laughable as a matter of history, but it's no less plausible than traditional stories explaining the pervasiveness of evil. Though I'm wary of challenging Biblical narratives, there's greater empirical support for seventeenth century slave ships than for a tree of knowledge, a talking snake, or the Garden of Eden. Original sin is original sin. Its stain remains even when the direct perpetrators have long since faded into memory.

Some beliefs require faith, and it's wrong for non-believers to insist that the faith of others conform to the contours of the historical record or boast empirical support. The Woke are entitled to the same indulgence we accord to other faiths. Or at the very least, they will become entitled to it when they concede that theirs is a faith, and that much of what they profess requires faith to believe. As long as they insist that their assertions rest upon factual and historical bases, we have every right to insist that they use standard definitions, long-accepted meanings, actual facts, and the historical record. On those bases, the overwhelming majority of Woke assertions fall flat.

All Americans can agree with the Woke that actual racism is evil. After all, actual racism runs afoul of America's most basic spiritual tenet, namely "that all men are created equal." Racism, however, is far from synonymous with evil. The world, sadly, is overrun with evils that have nothing to do with race. Contra intersectionality, many struggles are distinct. Though all exploitation hinges upon the identification of difference, not all differences are equal. In the history of America, race has been the most common distinction forwarded to justify discrimination. In the history of the world, however, religion, tribe, and language have been far more common.

Evil abounds, evil is real, and the ability to recognize evil appears to be a deep spiritual need. The Woke, most of whom deny the entire realm of spirituality, and even more of whom have rejected the collected wisdom of the ages enshrined in mature faith traditions, had to find it somewhere. They found it in sociology. Because Wokeism needs racism, however, it cannot let the rest of us transcend it. That's why the most vocal of the Woke antiracists reject the teachings of Martin Luther King, Jr. In Woke ideology, racism can only disappear once we've reached utopia. The Woke cannot allow it to disappear sooner, for that would undermine the deliverance they have not yet brought.

This reasoning has a clear parallel in an esoteric corner of Judaism. There are a few Chasidic sects—you can see members of the tiny, radical, antisemitic fringe known as the *Neturei Karta* appearing with Iranian mullahs and Hamas terror-supporters—who reject Zionism on religious grounds. In their view, only Messianic deliverance can restore legitimate Jewish sovereignty. Because the Jewish Messiah has not yet arrived, Jewish sovereignty runs counter to God's will. The State of Israel may thus appear to be a Jewish restoration, but in their religious judgment it's a heresy. (The *Neturei Karta* members buddying up to the mullahs and terrorists give an undeserved bad name to the many Torah-observant Jews voicing theological unease with Zionism—a movement grounded in nationalism rather than in Torah. Nearly all members of this camp exhibit a deep concern with the safety and Jewish life of the world's largest Jewish community, and thus support the State of Israel despite their theological qualms. A representative view comes from a story, possibly apocryphal, about a campaign stop New York City Mayor John Lindsay made to visit the anti-Zionist Satmar Rebbe. Before speaking, Lindsay sheepishly conceded that he usually touted his support for Israel to Jewish audiences but appreciated that such a sentiment would be misplaced among Satmar Chasidim. The Satmar Rebbe replied "We have a specific theological reason for opposing a Jewish state. A gentile who opposes the world's only Jewish state is just an antisemite").

To the Woke, the great steps America has taken toward a colorblind "content of character" society are similarly heretical. To the Woke, assertions that America has transcended racism—or even can and will transcend racism—land the same way a Christian might hear the assertions that humanity can and will transcend evil. All such claims resound in the voice of Satan—the trickster. They are shams made to look egalitarian and non-racist, but they serve mostly to instill false consciousness and impede our progress towards the true Woke utopia. Only a constant highlighting of the problem can help. Furthermore, given that racism is unavoidable, only an antiracist thumb on the oppressed side of the scale can provide any sense of balance.

Racism is perhaps the central theological concept of Wokeism. Its importance cannot be overstated. Which is precisely why those of us who adhere to more traditional faiths must understand what the Woke mean when they shout about it.

11. The Virus that Keeps on Giving

For the Woke, Covid was a godsend. Or rather, it would have been a godsend had Wokeism conceded the existence of a god. Given that few of the Woke are willing to do so and even fewer accept the notion of a sentient god capable of giving things, the arrival of Covid necessitated a somewhat different metaphor. Perhaps it was merely the gift that kept on giving. Either way, Covid provided Wokeism with two things central to the emergence and spread of a young faith: A community-forging epic and a rich source of ritual.

The epic part is clear. To the Woke, Covid was a plague of Biblical proportions. Only through the concerted effort of noble bureaucrats and credentialed experts—the primary fonts of Woke wisdom and morality—were we able to defeat it. The experience did more than demonstrate the inherent virtue and Truth of Wokeism. It forged a community of the Woke. We were all in it together! Those who FOLLOWED THE SCIENCE made it through unscathed. The skeptics and deniers fared poorly. Mississippi and Alabama—two of the least Woke states—posted the highest number of Covid deaths per million! The Science is Great!

Back in reality of course, not only was Covid *not* a plague of Biblical proportions, it never threatened to become one. Early worst-case scenarios operating with weak data and unrealistic assumptions—say, the notorious Imperial College Model of early 2020—projected that 4% of those infected would die. While 4% of a global population exceeding eight billion is a staggering number, a bit of perspective is in order. Europe's last major bubonic plague outbreak wiped out 25% of London in less than six months in 1665. If you want to get literally Biblical, the tenth plague eliminated every first-born Egyptian male.

Perhaps more to the point, the 4% forecast was an entirely unrealistic, absolute worst-case prediction of what might happen if the world ignored the virus entirely and everyone got infected. Anyone with any background in data integrity and statistical modeling—even without specific knowledge of epidemiology—could have poked enormous holes in the model (as many of us did). Marginal improvements to the model and modest mitigation efforts would have brought the projections, and more importantly the actual numbers, far lower; the Great Barrington Declaration pointed the way.

The truth was known early on. There were clear categories of vulnerability for which the infection-fatality rate *might* have reached 4%. For the population at large the rate was well below 1%. For otherwise healthy children it was statistically indistinguishable from zero. No matter. Governments around the world declared emergencies, suspended rights, imposed discriminatory rules, coerced vaccinations, and incarcerated citizens. Polls repeatedly show that among the most Woke communities, perceptions of the death rates were orders of magnitude greater than reality.

The Wokest of the Woke surveyed the carnage and declared themselves pleased. Woke globalists were positively giddy: Klaus Schwab's *The Great Reset* extolled these reactions as collective government action at its very best. His *The Great Narrative* sequel proposed deploying similar approaches to combat the looming climate apocalypse.

Anthony Fauci, the weaselly bureaucrat from central casting, became a heroic figure. The constancy of his predictions of imminent doom and his casual dismissal of long-revered freedoms and rights were rivaled only by the inconsistency of his prescriptions. New York Governor Andrew Cuomo, who held relatively calm press conferences while sending record numbers of the vulnerable elderly to their deaths, was another early Woke favorite—though his star dimmed a bit when news of his improper advances toward female subordinates began to burst forward. To the Woke, massive deaths are excusable to a man capable of showing up the dread President Trump; allegations of harassment are a step too far.

To the Woke, it's irrelevant that U.S. government overreaction almost certainly resulted in far more deaths—at far elevated costs and massive avoidable collateral damage—than would have a more measured response. In fact, much of the Woke-owned media space labels all such discussions "misinformation," or (on a generous day) misleading and irrelevant.

No, Wokeism required a plague of Biblical proportions for its experts to overcome, and so a plague of Biblical proportions it found. That Woke experts almost certainly made things worse rather than better is equally unimportant. Whatever the facts may have been, whatever the future may reveal, the status of Covid in Woke mythology is secure.

The mythological benefits of massive government overreaction, however, pale in comparison to Covid's contribution to the ritualistic aspects of Wokeism. A faith tradition without rituals is unsustainable. Rituals serve as the "secret handshakes" that bind the faith community while differentiating believers from non-believers. Rituals also provide the bridge between the earthbound faithful and spirit realm of the unknowable. Perhaps in part because the Woke refuse to see themselves as a faith community, however, their belief system had produced relatively few unifying rituals—until Covid.

For those who still doubted that Wokeism is a full-blown religion, the ritualization of public health during Covid demonstrated the case cleanly. While it's unclear which of the myriad Covid rituals will withstand the test of time, the enormity of the experience provided many rich opportunities. Consider, for example, the practice—popular in Woke communities during the shutdown's earliest days—of sanitizing mail, groceries, shoes, and anything else arriving in the home from the outside world. While the Woke themselves insist that they were doing little more than spraying Lysol to kill germs, their actions were easily recognizable as standard purification rituals.

The idea that the "outside" world—whether beyond the private home or merely beyond the control of the faithful—contains impurities is quite common among history's faith communities. Because no faith community willingly brings impurity into its midst but every community values items or people originating elsewhere, there must be some mechanism for removing the impurity. Gestures, incantations, and blessings are all common. So too is contact with a purifying substance, such as holy water. Trademark law be damned! A modern faith can absolutely deploy Lysol as its holy water—and Purell as an intense form of purification applicable to body parts rather than mere objects.

The practice of stopping all commerce at your front door, declaring it potentially or likely impure, putting it in contact with a purifying agent, then declaring it fit for household use is hardly new. It is, as is much of

Wokeism, a translation of standard faith concepts into contemporary pseudoscientific language. In the ancient world, our ignorant, superstitious, spiritual ancestors might have stopped commerce at the entrance to their encampments, declared it potentially or likely impure, sprinkled it with holy water, then declared it fit for community use—but that's because they were ignorant and superstitious. The modern, enlightened, Woke elite would never adopt such a mindless practice. Unless and until, that is, someone translated it into Woke-resonant language. "Impurity" is a concept for boobs and dullards. "Infection" is a different matter entirely.

That early purification ritual faded quickly from most homes and businesses. Today, only the most devout Woke establishments persist. All who visit such premises are impressed with their piety. Many among the Woke concede that they too should still be availing themselves of the added safety of uniform disinfectant. Like the faithful of all traditions, however, most of the Woke are content to defer purification to special events, braving the prospects of impurity on a day-to-day basis.

Covid purity even gave life to one of the most esoteric passages in the Bible: Leviticus's description of the travails of a leper. Upon signs of the first possible symptom, the potential leper must visit a priest. The priest runs tests to determine whether or not the symptom is indeed leprosy. If the test is negative, the patient is isolated at home for a week, then tested again. If the second test is also negative, a second week-long quarantine follows. If further tests remain negative, the priest declares the patient pure. If, however, any of the tests come back positive, the priest declares the symptom to have been leprosy. The leper is then banished, sent "outside the encampment," until the symptoms have disappeared. After a pre-set post-symptomatic period, a priest is called, tests are run, and the leper may be deemed suitable for readmission into society—after undergoing a purification ceremony.

Of course, our modern society could never engage in anything as old-worldly as a priestly determination of impurity using testing, isolation, quarantine, home care, banishment, retesting, declarations of fitness, or purification as a precondition for readmission to civil society. No, we run a strictly medical process of determining infection that deploys testing, isolation, quarantine, home care, banishment, retesting, and declarations of fitness as preconditions for readmission to civil society. Contemporary Wokeism bears no relationship to the purification codes of superstitious nomads beholden to prophets, priests, and an unseen God.

Of far greater durability than some of the purification rituals are the ritualized aspects of masking and vaccination. The face mask—the first sacred garb of Wokeism—never made any sense in the scientific world. A mask is a filter. Anyone who has ever encountered a filter understands that filters only filter if they're tailored to a task. To work, a face mask must have openings large enough to allow breathing but small enough to block particles of the undesired toxin. They must also be fitted and worn appropriately. A program requiring everyone to deploy a randomly chosen filter affixed in an arbitrary manner is a bad joke—at least as a matter of science. Furthermore, when the particles in question are spread via aerosol and the most common masks were either designed to block far larger particles or repurposed garments designed for warmth or fashion, the entire program makes its participants look ignorant and silly.

None of these observations were either secret or subtle. The government scientists promoting masking all knew them. So did every health care professional in the country. So did anyone who ever worked in construction, an industrial setting, or around chemicals. So did anyone who ever followed Martha Stewart's guidance in selecting just the right cheesecloth. I don't fall into any of those categories, and even I knew it.

Yet compliance—at least in select places and select times—was extraordinarily high. People tripped over themselves to demonstrate commitment to the cause. The rules of common courtesy inverted themselves. Though it had always been considered rude to comment on what other people, particularly strangers, were wearing, such old-style common courtesy flew out the window. The polite were those who adopted the new fashion trend with gusto. The truly righteous loudly condemned all within their purview who failed to conform. Yes, many of them knew that few of their masked neighbors had constructed a setup capable of preventing the aerosol-bound transmission of Covid, but even a poor filter blocks something, they reasoned. In an era of pandemic and panic, every little bit helps!

The belief became so strong and so widespread—prominent politicians, pundits, and celebrities staked their reputations on the virtues of masking—that many saw it as a form of mass psychosis. How else could anyone explain such widespread fidelity and authoritarianism in the name of a practice so obviously incapable of achieving its stated goal?

By now the answer should be obvious. The commitment to masking was spiritual, not psychotic. The notion that masks may do "something" to reduce communicable disease was likely true, but irrelevant. Forcing all women into burqas would likely reduce unwanted groping, but few campaign to force all American women into burqas. (Though I can recall when LAPD Chief Daryl Gates worked hard to stamp out the few pedestrian-friendly neighborhoods and events in 1980s Los Angeles as a way of reducing pickpocketing and jaywalking).

Somehow the argument was lost on mask advocates. And for good reason. Prior to the masks, there was no visible way for the Woke to identify themselves to each other. Masking gave them that—and more. Woke politicians sent them out to proselytize. Everyone must look Woke! Look Woke and you will become Woke! Walk the Woke and soon you will talk the Woke! You will feel the Woke! You will wake to the Woke! You will see that the Woke have saved you, and you will become one with the Woke.

Judaism has a similar concept: *mitoch shelo lishma ba lishma*. What is done for some reason other than for its own sake will soon be done for its own sake. Follow the religious commandments for selfish or utilitarian purposes, and you will soon come to embrace them for the sake of bringing yourself close to God. Why shouldn't Wokeism recognize the same path to righteousness? Wear the mask, mouth the mantras, and soon you too will experience true awokening.

Face masks served Wokeism in precisely the same way that all religious garb serves adherents to the faiths that adopt them. They identify and bond the community together. They serve as a reminder that all who wear them are united in their commitment to the common good. They bear a tenuous actual, but clear symbolic, relationship to the stated goal motivating adoption.

The deep spiritual attachment that many of the Woke developed for their masks became evident as mask mandates began to fade. The hysteria emanating from certain quarters—broadcast most amusingly on social media—reminded the truly Woke that they are far smaller in numbers than they like to believe. Those they had hoped to convert or coerce did what coerced converts always do when the coercion relaxes. They left the faith, discarded their religious symbols, and returned to their pre-existing lives.

The Woke attachment to face masks is unlikely to evaporate. Woke cities like New York and San Francisco are poised to join certain Asian cultures that have long donned face masks at the first sign of respiratory symptoms. Tourists to these fine cities (assuming that tourists return) a decade from now will likely report that there is always a smattering of locals wearing masks. Are they symptomatic? Are they afraid of contracting something? Or is it a symbolic expression of their underlying faith? The answers will blur. It won't matter. Locals will know the truth. Who was that masked man? I have no idea, but he must be piously Woke.

While face masks are a classic religious artifact, the Covid vax became a rite of passage. All decent people got themselves vaccinated at the earliest possible moment. Parents rushed to get their children vaccinated as soon as they were legally permitted to do so. Those with children deemed too young pleaded with the authorities to lower the age limit. They cheered every story of a pharmaceutical company announcing plans to secure legal permission. They tripped over each other to be the first to inject their young children with an experimental serum, conferring no conceivable medical benefit, for a disease that posed zero statistical risk to healthy children.

In a more rational moment these parents would have balked. Adoption was highest among elite helicopter parents, the sort that pore over ingredient lists to ensure that no unapproved preservatives or sweeteners enter their children's systems. Elite parents who research and compete and evaluate and monitor every aspect of their children's environment were the first to submit their children for medical experimentation.

Once again, their behavior seemed to border on the insane. Insanity, however, should always be the conclusion of last resort. Certainly, some of these parents acted out of terror. Others did it to conform with their

Woke neighborhoods, communities, and private schools. Most, however, did it because they recognized the vaccine as the precondition for full entry into the Woke flock—much like baptism for Christians, a *bris* for Jews, or any of the countless rites of passage that have arisen in nearly every tribe, faith, nation, or culture that history has ever recorded.

The Woke leadership sought to enforce their new rites with a coercive conversion far more intrusive, and with even weaker rationale, than mandatory masking. In fact, the greater the accumulated data suggesting that the vaccines were far less protective than originally thought, the harsher their coercion. New York City's very Woke Mayor Bill DeBlasio announced the country's first municipal vaccine passport requirement shortly after scientific data established that innocent bystanders could become infected with Covid from the vaccinated as easily as from the unvaccinated. As news of the vaccine's shortcomings mounted, the campaigns became increasingly hateful.

The vitriol America's Woke elite—from the Biden White House on down—heaped upon the unvaccinated was unprecedented. It may have been the first time in American history that the country's leadership sought to turn a majority of its citizens against a despised minority. Widespread discriminatory laws came into play for the first time since the end of Jim Crow. Prominent people advocated excommunication and the withholding of basic medical services—penalties that have never been seriously considered for smokers, the morbidly obese, helmetless motorcyclists, extreme athletes, or any of the other Americans whose personal choices make them likelier than average to require medical care.

The need to usher every living American—if not every living human—into the Woke covenant threatened to turn America into a hateful nation, flailing about seeking new ways to punish the selfish evildoers actively undermining our collective elevation of the common good.

Again, none of this makes any sense in any world other than a spiritual awakening. As the crusading missionary arm of a new faith, however, the Woke vaccine campaigns were rather mild. They even led to sectarian splits: Were those who took only the one-shot J&J adenovirus vaccination embraced on terms equal to those who demonstrated the commitment required for the two-shot, weeks long, mRNA ritual? How many vaccines were necessary for full admission to the flock? Did the rite of passage require renewal? What of a questioning convert who took the initial vaccination series willingly, but balked at the renewal ceremony known as the booster? Were they still part of the Woke flock? Had they become apostates—worse than those who had never entered the covenant at all? Is vaccination the sort of rite of passage the Woke must complete at least once in life? It is the sort that must be renewed? Is constant renewal merely a sign of devotion, with the truly pious running to be the first to each new booster and their less committed brethren allowed to lag?

Every new faith must grapple with such questions. And grapple the Woke did! Even many of the individual expressions of concern about Covid highlight its religious overtones. Consider a sentiment that was quite common, at least on social media:

The pandemic persists because of the unvaccinated. Their continued participation in society is a threat to us all. I have isolated as fully as possible, worn double and triple masks, gotten my full vaccination and booster the moment I became eligible, and I still got Covid. It was bad, but thanks to the vaccinations it wasn't worse. I survived and have mostly recovered, but something still feels off and I'm worried about long Covid.

In the scientific or medical realms, such statements are nonsensical. They describe people mired in deep anxiety who took ineffective (or at best, marginally effective) measures to mitigate an unavoidable airborne pathogen. Having still gotten sick, they blame their neighbors, show appreciation for failed vaccines, and emerge with a new source of anxiety.

In the religious realm, however, such sentiments are highly recognizable statements of faith. Consider a minor reformulation:

The plague persists because of the impure. Their continued participation in society is a threat to us all. I have distanced myself from them as much as possible, worn the sacred garments, committed fully to all rituals, and I still suffered the plague. It was bad, but thanks to The Science it wasn't worse. I survived and have mostly recovered, but my soul still aches as I ponder the future.

What had been a bizarre misunderstanding of science becomes a standard religious concern about the state of society, the persistence of divine intervention, the mystery of punishment falling upon the faithful, gratitude for the divine gift of personal salvation, and concern about the future.

At the end of the day, the Years of Covid have already played a critical role in the emergence of Wokeism: they provided plague, heroism, ritual, sacred garb, rite of passage, sense of community, the despised other, and more. Pre-Covid Wokeism was a rather threadbare religion. Post-Covid Wokeism is far richer and far better attuned to a broad range of spiritual needs. It is also more assertive, more coercive, more hateful of the "other," and more contemptuous of transgressors.

And it did it all without any reference to spirit, God, faith, or the unknowable. The Woke lexicon never once left the language of science. Even those of us who see the dangers of Wokeism should take a moment to marvel at its brilliance. It adapts even the most esoteric of spiritual needs to the language and metaphor with which its flock resonates.

12. The Moral Inversion

Is Wokeism really a religion? The answer hinges on a key definition: What is a religion? That's hardly an easy question. Nor is it an inconsequential one. While the First Amendment prohibits the establishment of a religion, it's silent on the establishment of ideologies or philosophies. It thus seems important to know where to draw the line between them. The Supreme Court has grappled with that challenge primarily from the perspective of people seeking religious accommodations despite their rejection of recognized religions, rather than people complaining that an official ideology being imposed upon them is a religion—Free Exercise claims rather than Establishment Clause claims. The Court's work towards an answer has been underwhelming, along the lines of its notoriously failed attempts to define pornography: We'll know it when we see it.

Consider the young men who sought conscientious objector status during the Vietnam War without belonging to a recognized pacifistic denomination. In those cases, the Supreme Court announced that "a religion" could arise from any sincere, meaningful belief parallel to the notion of a Creator—or even more generally, from any deeply held belief in core ethical principles. That expansive definition didn't long survive. The Court soon reeled it back—but failed to replace it with anything more coherent. Still, at least under that Vietnam War era definition, Wokeism makes the cut. The imposition of Woke "Truths" in schools, courts, or legislatures should violate the First Amendment.

Assuming, however, that we're operating under the "we'll know a religion when we see it" standard, the next question is where we should be looking. Most people would likely point to two identifying characteristics of "a religion:" a moral code and a god. As with the unaffiliated pacifists, Woke morality is far more obvious than the Woke deity. The Woke obsession with "justice" would make little sense without an underlying moral code. Granted, much of Wokeism represents an inversion of Biblical ethics, but an inverted moral code is still a moral code. Only a moral inversion could see racist mobs burning down our cities as "mostly peaceful" while labeling concerned parents "domestic terrorists." To make the inversion even clearer, the parental concerns that most incense Woke bureaucrats have far more to do with the moral character of K-12 education than with academic standards.

The Woke moral code is thus worth understanding, from its deepest roots through its daily implications. Unlike the Biblical notion that we were created in the image of God, Wokeism sees nothing special or elevated about the human species. The Woke obsessions with abortion and climate, and the Woke sects elevating animal rights, rest upon a devaluation of humanity. Woke animal rights extremists are explicit in their equation of humans with all other species. Woke abortion extremists reduce a gestating human fetus to a mere clump of cells until shortly after the moment of live birth. Woke climate catastrophists happily impose enormous costs upon human societies in the name of speculative and dubious benefits to the planet. While concerns with animals, abortions, and climate are hardly restricted to the Woke, only the Woke see them as easy questions leading to moral absolutes and militant extremism. Not surprisingly, the costs of these moral absolutes—perhaps most clearly on climate—fall largely on the poor, as the überelite Woke priesthood exempts itself from the inconvenience of adherence. That too is a moral judgement.

Woke morality was on full display during Covid. The dehumanization of the "unvaxed," the glee at the demise of anyone who questioned the authoritarian agenda, the abusive masking and de-schooling of children, the insistence upon managerial-class comfort to the detriment of workers, the isolation of the sick and the elderly from their loving families, the derision heaped upon those who lamented the loss of "freedumb," the determination that traditional religious services were not essential activities, and the reintroduction of class markings forcing masked waitstaff to serve unmasked patrons were all profound assertions of morality. They also highlighted how Woke morality has evolved to cater to, and to fill the spiritual needs of, a particularly callous, detached nobility. The flight of Woke politicians from the oppressive regimes they had imposed upon the masses to vacation in freer jurisdictions drove home the extent to which those in charge of Woke morality exempt themselves from its strictures. No surprise then that, through it all, the Woke spent every waking moment commending themselves on their own enlightened compassion and self-sacrifice, while complaining bitterly about the dangers they had to face thanks to the selfish, ignorant, deplorable, science-denying reactionaries living among them. The Woke see themselves as paragons of morality. That they had to invert morality to achieve that exalted status is of little moment.

Wokeism manifests its proudly inverse morality even more powerfully vis-a-vis children. In the Woke moral universe, good parents instill deep anxieties in their children, teaching them to become fragile, hypersensitive, self-entitled, spoiled, disrespectful, self-indulgent, overmedicated victims. Parents attempting to inculcate self-awareness, personal responsibility, internal discipline, openness, respect, trust, curiosity, or a love of freedom—or even simply trying to prevent the chemical sterilization and surgical mutilation of their children—risk having their children taken from them and turned against them. Interracial couples raising biracial children are immediately suspect, as are those who've adopted a child of a different race; their tenuous hold on their own children is subject to challenge on demographic grounds should they ever find themselves in a custody dispute. Woke educators systematically destroy independent thought, research skills, critical thinking, self-respect, and the free exchange of ideas—instead favoring doctrine, dogma, self-loathing, and a designation of all who dare question them as blasphemous haters unworthy of hearing or consideration. The Woke children they brainwash are then encouraged turn on the values their parents hold dear, enlist the support of Woke authorities, and win—shattering family dynamics and rendering effective, decent parenting impossible.

The moral inversion is widespread. Down the line, in story after story after story, normal decent people are vilified, punished, and sacrificed on the altar of Woke morality. Those elevating basic decency, common sense, human freedom, longstanding values, and a respect for tradition are increasingly cast as dangerous, oppressive, extremist reactionaries—if not as fascists or terrorists. With increasing regularity, basically decent people find the deck stacked against them in conflicts or altercations large and small, public and private, physical and litigious. Woke culture, media, and law all put a thumb on the scale in favor of those claiming preferred demographics, advocating anti-traditional ideas, imposing authoritarian solutions, separating loving parents from their children, radicalizing the youth, inculcating a broad sense of entitlement, and casting their abysmal behavior as retributive justice. The moral judgments are clear, consistent, and almost uniformly backwards. In many cases, even the symbolism is inverted. From the dawn of recorded history until 2016, kneeling was universally recognized as a sign of submission. That year, Colin Kaepernick kneeled in defiance of our national anthem. His Woke co-religionists quickly followed suit.

Woke "compassion" for those living in horrible conditions beyond our borders eliminates from consideration the most humane and successful programs ever devised: Permanent resettlement in countries and communities that share their culture, ethnicity, language, and religion. The Woke reject all such proposals immediately as "ethnic cleansing" or "genocide." Far more compassionate, the Woke insist, to turn these unfortunates into permanent human shields (e.g., the residents of Gaza) *de facto* invasion forces (e.g., the Syrian influx into Europe), or the property of human traffickers, rape gangs, extortionists, and drug cartels (e.g., at our southern border). That third group then gives the Woke an opportunity to make their uniquely inverted morality even clearer. Wokeism eagerly accommodates illegal arrivals with largesse far beyond anything available to American citizens in need—inverting a bedrock, previously universal moral rule that the obligations you owe to "your own people" (however you may define them) exceed those that you owe to others.

The compassion the Woke thus deploy to perpetuate, heighten, export, spread, import, and draw closer misery is hardly an anomaly. Many Woke deconstructions preserve the names of virtues while inverting the virtues themselves. The Woke define "gender affirmation" as helping boys pretend to be girls—and vice versa. They define a "book ban" as exercising discretion to remove graphic sexuality and brutality from school libraries and curricula. They define "academic freedom" as preserving classrooms, departments, and entire disciplines dedicated to fostering a single Woke viewpoint as Truth while labeling everything else hateful ignorance undeserving of an airing. They define "misinformation" as anything (true or false, known or unknown, opinion or fact) that might cause people to question an official Woke narrative. In point of fact, Wokeism denies biological reality on gender, bans books exhibiting traditional sensibilities, strangles free academic discourse, broadcasts grossly inaccurate information, and casts dubious opinion as unassailable fact. No matter. Having deconstructed and inverted the language, the Woke can claim the moral high ground—and they do.

The Woke are doing far more than playing word games to win a propaganda war. The Woke see themselves as profoundly moral—in fact, as history's first truly moral force. Wokeism judges everyone who has ever lived using contemporary Woke ethics—and finds nearly all severely lacking. The Woke moral code advocates rewriting history, toppling statues, and editing or removing all books written more than a decade-or-so ago as having reflected and promoted dangerous sensibilities. This behavior derives from a thought process paralleling the very traditional Islamic concept of the *jahilliyah*, the "age of ignorance" preceding Koranic revelation when humanity lacked the moral understanding necessary to live in accordance with God's will.

Yet Woke morality is as distant from the Koran as it is from the Bible. In an inversion that would shock adherents of any traditional moral code (though perhaps not those chafing beneath authoritarian legal regimes claiming fidelity to traditional moral codes), Woke morality is more a function of the actor than of the action. Much Woke morality flows from the belief that restoring balance and justice requires an intense focus on difference—and a consequent elimination of behavioral standards for those designated "oppressed."

To the Woke, the colorblind ethos that powered the Civil Rights movement—King's elevation of content of character over color of skin—is merely a pretext to perpetuate oppression. Thus, Black Rights Matter (BLM) seeks to improve the quality of black lives by: Eliminating the police charged with keeping black neighborhoods safe; reducing the schooling choices available to black parents (other than the very wealthy); deterring outside investment in black communities; curtailing programs for training, apprenticeship, internship, and employment; downplaying the importance of black churches; completing the evisceration of the black family; heightening the sense of black entitlement; and denying the existence of black agency. The righteous passion directed towards this agenda has led Woke mobs to destroy minority-owned businesses and business districts across America—in the name of racial justice.

Such Woke inversions stretch from street mobs to the chambers of power. When Congress asked a panel of three Woke priestesses—the Presidents of Harvard, MIT, and the University of Pennsylvania—whether those calling for genocide of the Jews violated their campus harassment policies, they testified that the question was unanswerable without knowing more about context. Why? Because in the Woke moral universe, a "white" student wearing a swastika T-shirt calling for genocide would be in violation; a "student of color" wearing a Palestine T-shirt spouting an identical message would not. Why? Because the barons of intersectionality have designated the Jews as historical oppressors while "Palestine" and "people of color" are oppressed. "White" students and neo-Nazis, like the Jews, are parts of the undifferentiated oppressor class. Thus, any anti-Jewish action emanating from the oppressed is justifiable as a blow for liberation and justice. Anything the Jews might do to deter or to retaliate against even the most barbaric such acts would be illegitimate. Intra-oppressor squabbles between Jews and Nazis—like the Holocaust—are inconsequential footnotes to the broad story of historical oppression.

The priestesses on that panel were savvy enough to appreciate that a clear answer would reveal the moral inversion of Wokeism in a manner unsuitable for public consumption. When Whoopi Goldberg had accidentally let the truth slip on *The View*—clarifying that "racism," as the Woke had deconstructed and redefined the term, had played no role in the Holocaust—she had to enlist the aid of Jonathan Greenblatt, the hopelessly Woke National Director of the hopelessly Woke ADL, to clean up her mess and restore the veil with which Wokeism shrouds its moral code. Seeing through that shroud, however, is becoming increasingly easy. To the Woke, the identity of an actor is far more relevant to moral judgment than is the action.

It gets worse. Under Critical Theory and "antiracism," the perpetuation of group difference, the subversion of the individual to the group to which they've been consigned, the heightening of sensitivities to the characteristics making each group distinct, and the presumed fragility of the traditionally oppressed are essential steps on the only moral path toward true social justice. Yet never—in any historical era, in any part of the world, or in any culture—has it benefited any identifiable minority to rivet majority attention on the things that make it different. To the contrary, that sort of heightened focus is invariably a precursor to atrocity. The Woke contention that an obsessive focus on difference benefits minorities runs so strongly counter to the entirety of human experience that only a deep and abiding faith could explain it.

Prior to the aspirational American notion that all men are created equal, most societies functioned as collections of semi-autonomous unequal groups. Whether the defining difference was faith, language, tribal affiliation, racial characteristics, or something else, those that the dominant group defined as "other" functioned on the fringes of society. They typically lived in their own villages or neighborhoods, faced restrictive opportunities in employment, mixed with the majority at their peril, operated subject to lesser legal protections, paid higher taxes or protection money for the privilege of existing, and had little recourse in the face of the occasional atrocity. The proper term for all such systems is "supremacist." Wokeism appears to have introduced a genuine innovative twist to this ancient construct: While some societies justified their condescending paternalistic supremacism as necessary because the "lesser" groups were unable to care for themselves, only Wokeism thought of championing supremacism as necessary to elevate the formerly downtrodden. It's hard to imagine a moral stance more inverted than positing supremacism as a remedy for oppression—but the Woke keep on trying.

To the Woke, as to all supremacists, individuals are merely representatives of their group or class. Moral judgments flow from generalized narratives rather than from individual action. Brett Kavanaugh's prominence traumatizes anyone who may ever have imagined that rich prep-school boys rape women with impunity. George Floyd embodies every black man ever mistreated by authorities while Derek Chauvin channels very one of those authorities. Specifics are entirely irrelevant. What matters are the narratives that these characters evoke. A consideration of specific actions and motivations might reveal unwanted nuance and complexity. Reducing the actors to caricatures guarantees moral clarity—and clarity is the key to justice. Woke lynch mobs outside the Chauvin trial brought the desired guilty verdict; the veiled Senatorial threats against Kavanaugh failed to derail his nomination.

This dismissal of specific action in favor of useful narrative recurs daily—particularly for those living in America's many Woke cities. In my own hometown of New York, Jose Alba was working hard in his bodega when the much younger Austin Simon burst in to attack him. Alba defended himself; Simon died. Woke city officials arrested and indicted Alba. Shortly thereafter, the mentally disturbed Jordan Neely threatened and endangered a full subway car; Daniel Penny bravely restrained him. Neely died. The city arrested, indicted, and arraigned Penny. In the Woke moral universe—reflected in official action, much of the media and social media—demographics alone determined that Simon and Neely were the worthy parties, Alba and Penny the villains.

New York is hardly unique. America's greatest cities are racing to the bottom. Decent residents of urban America—many of whom can scarcely imagine living anywhere other than the heart of a vibrant city—are learning that they've become unwelcome, unwanted, and unsafe in their own homes. To the extent that they've held onto their lifestyles, livelihoods, and families unscathed, it's mostly a matter of luck. Should they ever find themselves in a conflict, they'll discover that in Woke jurisdictions, most hallmarks of decency now represent moral black marks.

Woke morality has become so perverse that it imbibes and takes ownership of the atrocities of others. On October 7, 2023, Gazans led by Hamas militants—none of whom were remotely Woke—broke through into Israel and staged a horrific pogrom. They raped and tortured, disemboweled pregnant women, massacred babies, mutilated dead bodies, and engaged in acts so depraved that they beggar the imagination. They livestreamed it, boasted about it, and returned home conquering heroes to an adoring public. The 1400 dead, the 240 hostages, and the countless wounded and traumatized included many devoutly Woke victims.

Unlike the Nazis, who had taken pains to hide their atrocities, these Islamists broadcast their barbarism as points of pride. Why? Because Hamas—like its fellow Islamists in al Qaeda and ISIS before it—was out to reach the Western Woke. These barbaric terrorists understood that under the Woke moral code, the day's atrocities were fully justifiable in the cause of decolonization, particularly when deployed against Jews.

The Woke did not disappoint. They rallied to the terrorists' cause and cheered their noble efforts. The Woke/Islamist alliance took to the streets to show support. Its antisemitic mobs massed in cities and on college campuses across America—and across the West. When faced with a very hot war between the forces of civilization and the forces of barbarism, the Woke—from a safe distance, of course—called for the victory of barbarism, the preservation of the terrorist regime, the continued treatment of large populations as human shields, the promotion of genocide, the perpetuation of instability, and the destruction of conditions capable of leading to peace. They then proclaimed themselves uniquely moral for having taken such a bold stance.

Meanwhile, a disturbing number of Americans who'd proven impervious to prior Woke pieties dusted off their antisemitic bona fides to find common cause with the Woke, the terrorists, and the Islamists—in many cases for the very first time. In a theme that has recurred far too often in societies on the brink of self-immolation, hatred of the Jews unites strange bedfellows—foretelling very dark days ahead, not only for America's Jews but for all of American society.

It also portends a dilemma that everyone living in a Woke jurisdiction will eventually face: It's inherently unsafe to embrace *any* traditional notions of decency or *any* identity other than those on the intersectional list of the oppressed. When the Woke/Islamist alliance marching through American cities takes the next step and imports Gaza's groundbreaking terror techniques, will its new anti-Woke cheerleaders write off decent urban Americans as deserving of whatever they get, just as they have written off Israel's Jews? The schadenfreude emanating from some anti-Woke circles towards those trapped in America's rapidly imploding cities suggests that many will.

These newly emboldened anti-Woke antisemites are yet another symptom of America's spiritual crisis. When the enemies of decency declare a battle to the death, spiritually strong Westerners do what is necessary to win—as they did during the Second World War. Only the spiritually starved wonder whether it really matters which side emerges victorious as long as they can find personal safety on the sidelines. The surge of anti-Woke antisemitism, though far less elemental than surging Woke antisemitism, is yet another sign that much is wrong with the American soul. It's also a reminder that many Americans to whom Wokeism does not resonate have nevertheless abandoned the American Spirit. They may reject Wokeism, but they find themselves ambivalent when faced with the most gruesome example yet of the Woke moral inversion.

October 7th opened the floodgates—not only for antisemitism, but for terror support, blatant anti-Americanism, and the Woke/Islamist alliance more generally. By year's end, Osama bin Laden had emerged as a youth favorite on TikTok thanks to the many fine points he'd raised in his Letter to America justifying 9/11. Connecting those dark dates of spectacular terrorism is critical to appreciating the displacement of Western values by Wokeism. When al Qaeda struck in 2001, the entire Western world recognized its action as evil. By 2023, Woke westerners found such evil uplifting. In 2001, the few Westerners cheering al Qaeda were ostracized as dangerous, self-loathing moral degenerates. By 2023 their formidable movement highlighted Western civilizational decline. The antisemitic mobs could not have emerged as they did without unvetted (often illegal) immigration, decades of tacit bipartisan support for Islamism, and the commanding heights of Wokeism. The Woke moral inversion is becoming bolder, prouder, and increasingly bloodthirsty. In a pattern that has repeated itself with disgusting regularity over the course of centuries, what began as overt antisemitism threatens to become Wokeism's first Holy War.

Are those of us who still cling to the American Spirit up for the challenge? Perhaps we are. After all, we have God on our side. We must have God on our side because we're the only ones who want to be on God's side. Most Woke recoil at the mere mention of God; the rest recoil at the idea that God might intervene or take sides in human affairs. Yet, to return to the question of whether Wokeism is a religion, the Woke aversion to God hardly implies that Wokeism rejects the concept of a deity—or in the words of the Supreme Court, a deeply held belief that parallels the notion of a Creator.

In fact, the existence and scope of the Woke moral code compels at least such a parallel belief. Morality—judgments of good and evil—must come from somewhere. The Bible and the Koran derive them from the revelations of a monotheistic God. Jefferson credited them to a Creator and to Natural Law—Deist conceptions of that same monotheistic God. The emphatically atheistic Karl Marx sourced his moral code to the Dynamic of History. Woke morality cannot have arisen without a source. That source parallels the God whose revelations animated all monotheistic moral codes.

The seemingly strongest counterargument to the idea that Wokeism is a religion—namely the absence of any obvious Woke deity—thus collapses beneath the weight of Woke morality. The need for a moral code, and the consequent need for an unassailable font of morality existing above the human plane, seem to define fundamental human spiritual needs. Once again, those who walked away from the ways that traditional faiths meet these needs have found non-traditional ways to meet them. Westerners who thought they could live in a human-centric world of pure moral subjectivity failed—again without ever being forced to confront their failure. Wokeism has handed them a detailed moral code emanating from an infallible source that must remain unnamed and unimagined—a concept that Abraham himself would have recognized.

That conclusion brings us full circle. The central thesis of this entire inquiry is that today's America—and in particular today's American elite—is spiritually starved. Wokeism, I have posited, is spreading because it addresses their unarticulated spiritual needs. The Woke god, cast in the language and metaphor of literate, credentialed bureaucrats focused on the challenges of abundance, may remain implicit. That doesn't reduce its importance in the hearts of the faithful. Wokeism is a religion whose tenets provide deep meaning to its adherents while also meeting an increasing number of the spiritual needs they have buried and denied. For better or for worse, American culture, American society, and American law must start treating Wokeism as a religion. Anything else could cripple the American Spirit as ascendant Wokeism wages a full-blown Holy War against traditional morality.

III. THE AMERICAN SPIRIT UNDER FIRE

13. Never Without a Religion

How did America become mired in a spiritual crisis so deep that it undermines the very essence of our national identity? Through flawed interpretations of history, spirituality, and the constitution.

The zealously anti-religious view of the separation of church and state, the absence of a clear definition of "religion," and the consequent misinterpretation of the First Amendment have wreaked untold carnage upon American society. They have generated many conversations of deep policy significance that make no sense at all.

Take, for example, one of the central questions of the abortion debate: When does life begin? The idea that life begins at conception is widely considered "religious" because more than a few recognized denominations—notably the Roman Catholic Church—declare it as an article of faith. The idea that life begins only at birth, on the other hand, is rarely considered "religious" because few if any recognized denominations forward that position. Moreover, many of its loudest proponents claim to disdain religion and faith altogether. They assert it as an obvious scientific truth that those who've already been born alive are indeed alive, while those who have not been born are not alive. QED.

As common as such debates have become, however, they make no sense at all. The question "when does life begin" hinges upon the definition of life. As St. Augustine said about time, life is one of those things that we know when we see it, but the more we think about it the less we understand it. "When does life begin?" is an inherently metaphysical question. It has no demonstrably right or wrong answer. Common answers—including the appearance of a heartbeat or brain activity as well as the moments of conception and birth—are all plausible and justifiable. None, however, are demonstrably correct. Because the question itself veers into metaphysics, so too must the answers. Anyone who believes that there are meaningful lines separating metaphysics from spirituality from religion from faith is either ignorant or delusional. All answers to metaphysical questions are equally "religious."

The debate between those who argue that all abortion is murder because life begins at conception and those who argue that all abortions represent individual choices because life begins at birth is a debate between two different religions. It's as resolvable as any debate between the metaphysics of distinct faiths—in other words, not at all. From a policy perspective, the applicable questions should be: At what point should the law attach certain rights to an *in vitro* human? At what point during pregnancy has a woman been given a fair opportunity to make a decision for which she must bear responsibility?

Such questions would frame a rational debate about the status of a fetus and of abortion as questions of policy and law. They would avoid the metaphysics entirely. In a similar vein, the entire debate about gender dysphoria hinges upon a metaphysical belief that it's possible to be "born into the wrong body." In the physical world, we are each born into the bodies into which we're born. No question of "right" or "wrong" bodies is meaningful, or even possible. In the realm of metaphysics, spirit, or faith, however, many questions about the rightness, wrongness, arbitrariness, or unfairness of birth become possible.

The broader point, however, is that a full, clear division between church and state is impossible. No system—no society, no legal code, no country, no set of beliefs, no moral code—is possible without resort to metaphysical questions or answers grounded in faith. The Declaration of Independence asserts that governments are man-made institutions whose purpose is to secure inalienable rights. As a result, the Constitution is a man-made document that does not reference God. Fair enough, but if the Constitution derives its legitimacy from its efforts to secure inalienable rights, what's the source of those rights and what makes them inalienable? The answers to such questions lie entirely in metaphysics.

No society can exist without some notion of morality, and empirical observation alone cannot provide values or morals. Only the metaphysical—or spiritual or religious—realm can do so. People or movements who pretend to rely exclusively upon pure empiricism must necessarily become nihilistic observers. Even the reputedly amoral quest for *la dolce vita*, placed in a values vacuum, is more accurately a quest for *dolce far niente*. After all, the very notion that hedonism is "better than" or "preferable to" asceticism implies a value judgment. Dionysius too was a god.

Because every system needs at least one axiom, no system can exist without at least a modicum of faith. Martin Luther King Jr.'s friend and compatriot Rabbi Abraham Joshua Heschel noted: "Every one of us is bound to have an ultimate object of worship, yet he is free to choose the object of his worship. He cannot live without it; it may be fictitious or a real object, God or an idol." Evolutionary theorists don't understand everything about evolution. Cosmologists can't explain why the big bang happened when it did or how it did. No one has any firm idea what creates "life," where it comes from, and what happens when it ends—and those who claim to know are typically flummoxed when asked for empirical support. Few who elevate empirical science above all concepts of God can explain the source of science. And those who claim to rely upon logic and thought alone to define morality are often unwilling or unable to reveal the axioms that underpin their value systems—much less the source of those axioms. During Covid, those who admonished us to "Follow The Science" were as resistant to questions as any of history's greatest anti-blasphemy crusaders.

Even in the modern world, some questions remain unanswered; to us, they appear unanswerable. If and or when we answer them, newly unanswerable questions will take their place. And so, we find ourselves once again on the horns of a timeless dilemma: Do we ignore such questions because they appear unanswerable? Or do we accept an underivable answer as an axiomatic article of faith? Invariably, we choose to axiomatize our answers, much as our ancestors have done from time immemorial.

In the modern world, many people eschew the language of "God" and "faith," favoring instead the terminology of "scientific fact" and "logical derivation." This choice is particularly pronounced among those who consider themselves enlightened, secular, humanist—and Woke. Most such people pride themselves on having rejected the specific concept of God—and the accompanying sets of rituals—that their background handed them. For today's Woke, that represents a rejection of Americanism and of Biblical morality.

To a very large extent, however, what most bothers these rejectionists is the notion of a sentient, teleological god. In the Biblical tradition as in many (if not all) faith traditions, God created the world for a purpose. God had a reason for allowing evil to exist, and at times to flourish. God rewarded and punished as part of a plan. Depending on the culture and the circumstances, gods could be noble or petty, compassionate or vindictive, vengeful or merciful, intentional or whimsical. Gods could squabble among themselves, limit each other's power, and suffer from unintended consequences. Followers of specific gods and faith traditions have committed numerous atrocities in the name of their gods. With such historical baggage, it's little wonder that those whose ultimate answer is simply "some force" prefer to avoid speaking of "god."

For the Woke, that force is enlightened elite opinion, expert analysis, or The Science. For other anti-theists it may lie elsewhere. In all of their allegedly anti-religious systems, however, the role that their force plays is identical to the universalistic conception of god. At the heart of every belief system—theistic, non-theistic or atheistic—lies a core axiom. Ask the believers to identify the source of that axiom, and they will flounder. The answer, of course, is the one that we have always given to such questions. That answer is "God," however defined—even to those who prefer "May the Force Be with You" to "God Bless You."

In short, neither the foundational American Spirit nor contemporary Wokeism can reasonably claim to be devoid of faith-based fundamentals. Because no state can function without some axiomatic faith-based morality, the complete division between church and state is impossible. What then, could the First Amendment's dual guarantees of Free Exercise and No Establishment mean? The answer isn't difficult: The First Amendment protects Americans from being forced to accept another faith's notions of right and wrong—and to conform individual behavior accordingly. The separation of church and state has nothing to do with shielding Americans from exposure to the ceremonies, rituals, or icons of a faith other than their own; public displays are a far cry from "establishment." More importantly, the separation was never designed to shield Americans from the notions of right and wrong embedded in the American spiritual platform. Those who suggest otherwise have trapped themselves in a logical impossibility; rejection of the platform necessarily includes rejecting the separation.

The First Amendment's view of the proper role of religion in American life, properly understood, is but part of a rich collection of beliefs. The Declaration overflows with faith-based assertions: All men are created equal? They are endowed by their Creator with certain unalienable rights? That among those rights are life, liberty, and the pursuit of happiness? That the thirteen American colonies are entitled to a separate and equal status?

All great statements. All meaningless outside the realm of faith. All faith-based assertions used to define what it means to be an American. All criteria so central to national definition that those who deny them cannot fairly claim to be Americans. Does that sound like a nation founded without an underlying religion?

Few if any of the foundational beliefs of Wokeism make any sense outside the realms of metaphysics, spirit, or faith, either. Slavery is immoral? I happen to agree, but the statement makes little sense in the absence of some spiritual or metaphysical basis for morality. Racism is wrong? Again, I agree fully, but what's the basis for defining "wrong?" It's possible to be born into the wrong body? I don't buy that one, but it does lead me to ask what defines the "right" or "wrong" body in which to be born.

Stated simply, the culture wars or political polarization roiling 2020s America are religious wars. We can pretend otherwise but we'd just be pretending. On one side sit a number of traditional denominations drawn from multiple faith traditions. On the other sit Wokeism itself, most other variants of utopian socialism, and some breakaway denominations still claiming disingenuously to belong to traditional faiths. The framing is clear, even if many would like to pretend otherwise.

A century ago, G.K. Chesterton called America "the only nation in the world that is founded on a creed." At the time, all European states recognized their ethnonational foundations. Blood, language, and shared historical experience defined those nations. The American nation stood alone on its creedal foundations.

How could such a nation determine who belonged and who did not? That's not a technical legal question of determining who qualifies for U.S. citizenship. It's a metaphysical, philosophical question that goes straight to the heart of what it means to be "an American."

The answer lies at the very start of the document that declared the American nation into existence: The Declaration of Independence.

The Declaration's establishment of a new creedal nation is hardly subtle. The language may have become too familiar to warrant notice, but it's worth pondering the meaning of "We hold these truths to be self-evident, that all men are created equal, that they are endowed by their Creator with certain unalienable rights, that among these are life, liberty and the pursuit of happiness."

There's nothing remotely self-evident about equality or rights. In all of human history prior to 1776, no society had ever organized itself along those lines. An actual "self-evident truth" is an assertion that few would bother debating, much less actively ignore. "That all men are created equal" doesn't come close to qualifying. Furthermore, if you really want to state a self-evident truth, why pump yourself up? "We hold?" Who cares what your opinion may be about a self-evident truth? You noticed something self-evident? Hardly worthy of bragging rights or lofty pronouncements. What in the world was Jefferson thinking?

A bit of close thought and textual analysis reveals the answer. Jefferson's curious phrasing is deeply profound. It's the creed that defined the new American nation. As with the core beliefs of all faiths or ideologies, certain axioms are "self-evident" only among the faithful. God gave the Torah to the children of Israel at Sinai? God sent His only Son to die for our sins? There is no God but God and Mohammed is His prophet? From each according to his ability, to each according to his needs? The arc of history bends toward justice? All are axiomatic truths among believers. Non-believers remain skeptical.

So too with the American Declaration. The defining creedal axiom of the American system is "that all men are created equal, that they are endowed by their Creator with certain unalienable Rights, that among these are life, liberty and the pursuit of happiness." Don't believe it? You're not an American. We wish you well, but you don't belong to our nation—even if you're a U.S. citizen.

Much as nations born of blood defend the blood, a nation born by creed must defend the creed. An American nation that renders its defining self-evident truths optional is an American nation on the brink of extinction. A creedal nation must demand fidelity to its foundational creed or it will dissipate into the ether.

Was the American nation founded without a religion? Of course not. A "religion" is little more than an expanded creed plus a set of rituals and practices. The American creed is far simpler, far shorter, and far less demanding than the creeds of any pre-existing faith traditions. It is, however, quite real. Full membership in the American nation may not demand much, but it does demand something. It demands fidelity to the basic defining creed of the Declaration of Independence.

Jefferson didn't create that creed from whole cloth; he extracted it from the core ethical foundations of the Bible and centuries of Anglo tradition. Per the Declaration, full membership in the American nation requires faith in a Creator, natural law, the inherent equality of all humans, and a set of individual rights. It recognizes no divine authority in government—a man-made entity whose sole purpose is securing those natural rights. It promises to welcome as equals all denominations capable of building upon that shared ethical platform. That creed defines America's spiritual underpinnings—the American Spirit.

14. The Beauty of a Spiritual Platform

This entire inquiry opened with a three-pronged argument: One, America is mired in a deep spiritual crisis. Two, Wokeism is a new religion, well attuned to our times, that has arisen to meet the spiritual needs of the most spiritually starved Americans. Three, only a revival of America's founding spirit can preserve the American nation and the American republic. All three prongs are critical.

While Wokeism was born denying its spiritual roots, the denial of the American Spirit is a recent misstep. For at least the first half of the country's existence, every American understood that our national founding was a profoundly religious act. The American nation was founded, quite intentionally, with an incomplete, skeletal religion. The Declaration of Independence is replete with references to a "Creator," "natural law," and "rights." Such beliefs may be shared widely, but they're not remotely universal. Any faith comfortable with such basic beliefs may complete the American identity—allowing genuine, full Americans to manifest themselves in very different ways. Any denomination of any faith that rejects those beliefs is, by definition, incompatible with the American identity.

The American adoption of an intentionally incomplete creed as the core of its national identity was the first demonstration of American exceptionalism. Prior to that American declaration, most if not all societies had officially "established" religions that defined not only worship and holidays, but all aspects of culture and society. That all-encompassing view of the "state religion" persists in much of today's non-Western world—in ways that often confuse and confound Americans.

In contemporary terms, America's founding civic religion is a "platform" rather than a "system." That term, which I've used throughout this inquiry, defines an extraordinarily broad set of principles that its founders deemed essential for a coherent society. The American Spirit always assumed that all (or at the very least most) Americans would augment its basic platform with a more traditional faith.

Inherent in that assumption is the recognition that for many, faith affiliation is nominal. Others might veer clear of traditional faiths altogether, substituting secular organizations capable of meeting some of the spiritual and/or communal needs typically associated with religions. Over the years, fraternal orders, professional societies, bowling leagues, affinity groups, fan clubs, and social media chat groups have arisen to provide this completion—some with greater success than others. Alexis de Tocqueville, perhaps the first great outside observer of American society, testified to the extent to which early Americans turned this abstract goal into an effective reality.

How did those early Americans do it? Americans have long understood this relationship between platform and completion instinctively. Those of devout faith never saw their Americanism as a challenge to their Christianity, Judaism, Mormonism, Islam, Hinduism, Buddhism, etc. In fact, more saw it as an enhancing complement than as a competitor. Hyphenated Americans abounded, as those claiming personal or ancestral ties to a foreign culture imported the best of their ancestral cultures proudly, paired it seamlessly with their Americanism, and enhanced the American nation. Many others adopted alma maters, sports franchises, or organizational memberships as key parts of their identities—again, feeling that it enhanced rather than challenged their identities as Americans.

Without some core shared beliefs and values, however, no society can long cohere—as contemporary American society is demonstrating. Furthermore, like all faiths, the American spiritual platform incorporated aspirational elements. To this day, some of those elements remain aspirational. Imperfection of adherence—by individuals, by the American nation, and by the governments we have chosen to represent us—does nothing to negate underlying principles.

The American Spirit is thus incomplete by design. It was built as a foundational platform broad enough to embrace Americans arriving from every faith tradition of which the founders were aware—though not necessarily every denominational interpretation or every practice of every faith tradition. It presumed that most Americans would indeed adhere to a faith tradition, even if nominally, and that most of the remainder would seek connection, guidance, and completion in civil society organizations. Only the combination of that American platform and a faith tradition (or a civil substitute) could meet the full range of human ethical, spiritual, and communal needs.

The American innovation of a spiritual platform, based upon Biblical ethics, that simultaneously requires an additional system for completion and permits multiple such additions enabled interfaith dialogs unthinkable under most other systems. It became possible for Americans vested in the American Spirit to engage in a quest for similarities among faiths rather than—as has been far more common—for differences. In a very real sense, the American spiritual platform allows adherents of all faiths to cling tightly to their particularistic notions of "Truth" while sharing a quest for wisdom. Perhaps unsurprisingly, the Woke disdain the American incorporation of wisdom from other cultures, deriding this glorious virtue as "cultural appropriation." Rather than finding common ground and mutual admiration—the key to America's success—Wokeism emphasizes difference and promotes inter-group tension.

Americans have always been proud of this acculturation. Our spiritual platform was designed to extract, assimilate, and Americanize cross-cultural wisdom. Under no prior system was it possible to give equal footing to the deep insights that have helped the faithful of multiple faiths find meaning and purpose. Americans were not the first to appreciate that insight and wisdom knows no boundaries. In a philosophical moment that prevailed a thousand years ago, a rediscovery of Ancient Greek logic and reason, and its alignment with faith, reshaped the world. Aquinas imported Plato and Aristotle into Christian thought. Maimonides did the same for Jewish thought. Despite initial resistance, they became central thinkers who redefined and redirected the faithful—and the future of their faiths. Their centrality persists to this day. Averroes, their contemporary who did the same for Islam, received a colder reception. Many saw the imposition of reason and consequentialism as infringements of God's will. To this day, segments of the Islamic world reject the idea that poor outcomes emerge from poor human decisions rather than from divine will—complicating the efforts of many committed to the development and welfare of the Islamic world. The brilliant American innovation of a spiritual platform pushed hard in the opposite direction. It invited input from all sources, reasoning that the collected wisdom of the globe benefited from insights and circumstances that arose anywhere, rather than in one particular region, culture, or faith.

Only the wide-open American quest for wisdom could draw together: The Talmudic sage Ben Zoma's: "Who is wise? He who learns from all, for it is written 'from all my teachers, I gained understanding.'" Confucius's amplification: "By three methods we may learn wisdom: First, by reflection, which is noblest; Second, by imitation, which is easiest; and third by experience, which is the bitterest." Buddha's caveat: "Do not believe in anything simply because you have heard it. Do not believe in anything simply because it is spoken and rumored by many. Do not believe in anything simply because it is found written in your religious books. Do not believe in anything merely on the authority of your teachers and elders. Do not believe in traditions because they have been handed down for many generations. But after observation and analysis, when you find that anything agrees with reason and is conducive to the good and benefit of one and all, then accept it and live up to it." And Saint Paul's admonition: "If any of you think you are wise by the standards of this age, you should become fools so that you may become wise."

It's hard to imagine a warning better suited to 2020s America. In the twenty-first century, those who consider themselves wise by the standards of our age proclaim their willingness to learn from all *except* people of faith. Even prior to the rise of Wokeism and the denigration of "dead white males," America's elite enclaves overflowed with credentialed professionals fully comfortable quoting Shakespeare, Descartes, and Aristotle and finding wisdom selectively throughout the history of philosophy and literature—except in sacred scriptures.

That rejection marked an important step away from the American Spirit. Recall Jefferson's redacted Bible—pulling the miracles to make the case that even if Jesus were less than divine, his teachings contained much wisdom? The decades leading from that American spiritual ethos to Wokeism began when those who did not find personal inspiration in scripture felt compelled to denigrate it. They insisted that though scriptural texts have inspired billions of people for scores of generations, they're nevertheless devoid of wisdom worth learning—contra Ben Zoma. Why?

The Gospels provide the answer: Jesus came to his own country; and his disciples followed him. When he began to teach the people were impressed—but hardly complimentary. Who does this guy think he is? Where did he get this stuff? What makes him so wise? Isn't he a carpenter? Don't we know his family? Employing a technique well known in modern life, they dismissed Jesus's message because they found his credentials unimpressive. To which Jesus replied: "A prophet is not without honor, except in his own country, and among his own kin, and in his own house." Upon realizing that he couldn't teach effectively to people whose familiarity impeded their ability to take him seriously, Jesus healed a few sick people and headed out of town.

Though Ben Zoma and Buddha would both have disapproved of the crowd's behavior, it's precisely Jesus's hometown crowd that set the stage for the rise of utopian socialism—and ultimately of Wokeism. Biblical morality had become so familiar that many Westerners took it for granted. They moved away from the source of shared ethics, deemed it uniquely toxic because of its familiarity, and eventually slid into a belief system that views it as the worst of the world's various faiths.

The net result is the moral inversion of Wokeism. Viewed through a Biblical lens, Woke leaders encourage and empower their Woke flock to become the very worst versions of themselves, fully entitled to impose their will upon their neighbors in the name of the common good. As an anti-biblical tradition originating after the Declaration, the utopian tradition has already generated denominations and practices incompatible with Americanism—communism and fascism come immediately to mind. Wokeism, in its current configuration, with its current emphasis on imposing its beliefs and practices on all Americans, threatens to become another. If we want to reclaim our country, we're going to have to reconnect with the Biblical ethics at the beating heart of the American Spirit.

15. Living in the Material World

The appeal of Wokeism to America's elite is hard to miss. Using only the contemporary metaphors and scientific language with which they resonate, it provides answers to many of their spiritual questions:

Racism explains persistent unfairness and inequality far more tangibly than some amorphous sense of "evil." It relates to events within American historic memory and manifests itself in current events.

The Trans Movement enshrines the concept of an inner self, far truer than the physical shell of the body, capable of addressing questions of identity, individuality, and uniqueness—as well as those concerning existence before birth and after death. It does so using language far more concrete and pseudoscientific than references to an immortal soul.

Apocalyptic climate change spins an elegant tale of the end of days. It provides an organizing theme for an Armageddon worth avoiding, a call for repentance and reformation aligned with the prescriptions of the faith, and a vague set of predictions that can never be disproved. It achieves these tasks neatly, using only the language of science, without reference to anything as metaphysical as divine judgment or messianic deliverance.

Covid extremism handed this nascent religion a glorious gift. From inception, it arrived as a plague of biblical proportions that only the appointed, enlightened, elite experts could tame. Their various pronouncements and prescriptions gave rise to a wealth of religious markings and rituals.

Anti-misinformation campaigns and cancellation provide mechanisms for policing adherence to—or at the very least, recognition of—religious norms that sound far less archaic and draconian than do anti-blasphemy laws and excommunication.

The absence of an obvious deity is far less troubling than it might first appear to be. It is hardly unlikely that, at some point, some Woke faction will feel the need to define the originating source of Wokeism's various beliefs. For most believers, however, the devoted belief itself is far more important than its source. Every coherent system may require at least one axiom, but few people operating within any system pay more than fleeting attention to its axiomatization.

Wokeism thus fills many of the same spiritual needs that past humans have felt without forcing today's urban, credentialed, professional, elite sophisticates to delve into unrelatable pastoral metaphors or deep metaphysics. Nevertheless, it's doomed to fail because it's no better than traditional faiths at addressing the primary spiritual challenge of our time—abundance—and it's far less attuned to human nature.

The shift from a world of scarcity to a world of abundance is not a matter of "mere" economics. It's a defining inflection point in human history. It makes the modern world different from the pre-modern world in fundamental ways. The utopians, to their great credit, understood the significance of this change. Their error lay in believing that human nature could change to accommodate it.

Two centuries after the rise of utopianism, the challenge is coming to a head. Traditional faiths—all traditional faiths that have withstood the test of time—are finely attuned to human nature and human needs. The differences among faiths stem primarily from the emphases they place on different aspects of human nature. All surviving faiths have provided so much meaning and definition, to so many people, over so many changing circumstances and such lengthy periods of time, because they have tapped into something primal. It's unclear, however, that they've successfully navigated the transition to abundance. Their continued viability, coupled with their constant hemorrhaging of adherents, suggests that they've internalized some but not all parts of the transition.

Utopianism—in all its formulations, including Wokeism—has grappled with abundance far more explicitly and honestly than most traditional faiths. Marx's famous formulation—from each according to his ability, to each according to his needs—seems like eminently sensible morality in a world of abundance. If there is indeed enough to go around, how could it possibly be moral to deny anyone his needs?

The problem with the Marxist formulation is that it's impractical, not that it's immoral. As a practical matter, too few people will produce for the benefit of those who sit idle, waiting for global production to exceed global needs then simply claiming their share. Human nature—unchanged by abundance—guarantees that production will decline, needs will go unmet, and the world will slide back into scarcity.

Traditional faiths—including America's spiritual foundations—recognize humans but have not yet fully internalized the transition to abundance. Utopians understand abundance but have lost all sense of humanity. In a very real sense, the struggle of our time is the race to see who can address the reality of humanity operating in abundance first and best. Should all such efforts fail—a very real possibility—the world will likely collapse back into scarcity. The next round of battles will occur on very different terrain.

It's imperative that traditional faith denominations consistent with the American spiritual foundations prevail. Such an outcome is an absolute necessity for the continued welfare of humanity and the world at large. It is not, however, preordained. Even those whose faith in a divine plan is far more elemental than my own must concede that there are many surprising and disturbing blips on the road to ultimate salvation. Certainty that God will prevail in the long run says little about life during the times of our children and our grandchildren.

To prevail, traditional faiths will have to take a page from Wokeism while avoiding the trap that dooms Wokeism to failure: They will have to set aside pastoral language and metaphor while addressing the fundamental spiritual challenge of abundance. Can tradition—and the American Spirit—prevail?

Most traditional faiths—along with various schools of psychology—long ago noticed that fundamental challenge. Abundance does not bring happiness. It does not provide meaning. To the contrary, abundance seems to heighten depression and anxiety. The evidence is everywhere and decades of data back it up. You cannot shop or spend your way to a life of happiness and meaning. Acquaintances and hangers-on can be purchased; friends and community cannot. Abundance may pose the greatest spiritual challenge yet to confront a species evolved to overcome scarcity: Having won our ultimate battle and conquered our timeless enemy, we find the victory disturbingly hollow.

Logotherapy posits our internal struggle as the quest for meaning or purpose. Viktor Frankl's ability to extract this glorious theory from the ashes of Nazi concentration camps highlights the paradox. Prisoners at the camp, though far from all affluent, were all products of modern European abundance. What possessions they may have had—down to the clothes on their backs—were stripped from them. They entered the camps possessing only their bodies and their minds. The Nazis then worked to dispossess them of their bodies and break their minds. Frankl's key observation was that those whose minds clung tightly to metaphysical purpose and meaning were by far the most likely to survive.

Therein lies the problem. Prospect theory—from the very different corner of cognitive psychology—teaches that human utility functions have a inflection point at zero. In less technical terms, we're all far more afraid of losing what we already possess than of failing to gain what we might want. Consider a simple hypothetical. If I told you of an investment strategy capable of doubling your net wealth within three years, would the thought make you happy? Most normal people would answer yes. Now here it is in practice: In year one, I will double your net wealth. In year two, I will double it again. In year three, I will cut it in half. The net result is that in three years, your net wealth will be double what it is today—and you will be deeply miserable. Guaranteed. The moment you internalized your year-two ending wealth quadruple where you are today, it became part of you. Clawing back half of it ripped a hole in your sense of self.

Positive psychology makes the matter even clearer: The richer a society becomes, the higher the rates of depression and anxiety. Abundance can make us fat. It cannot make us happy. Positive psychology also, however, points us back in the right direction. Gratitude and acknowledgment can increase happiness. In other words—to the surprise of no traditional faith—happiness is elusive in the material realm but accessible in the spiritual realm.

Bhutan, the only country to establish Varjayana Buddhism as its official state religion, has developed the "Gross Domestic Happiness" (GDH) index to measure collective happiness and well-being—and set GDH maximization as an explicit national goal. While non-Buddhist nations might need to adjust some of the underlying philosophies and measurements, the concept speaks loudly to a world whose elevation of the tangible and measurable—and consequent exclusion of the spiritual — has left the vast majority of its citizens disconnected, joyless, and searching for meaning.

Therein lies the great spiritual challenge of our time—a challenge that Wokeism is singularly unable to meet. In a world of scarcity, we humans have no choice but to look inward. In a world of abundance, the outside world always has something tantalizing to offer. As that outside world expands, so too do its distractions. We have become so attuned to our possessions that we are rapidly losing the skills that made us human.

Start with the classic Marxist formulation—or even just its second half. "To each according to his needs" breeds a sense of entitlement. Entitlement is an entirely modern innovation, born in a world of abundance. All traditional societies embraced a sense of obligation. Royals, nobles, priests, and the wealthy were all obliged to care for the community. Charity networks existed within every faith, culture, and tribe. While no poor person could ever stand in the middle of town demanding entitlement to food or shelter, a town that let its poor suffer from starvation or exposure was a town without honor. That sense of communal dishonor is ancient. It appears in the esoteric Biblical discussion of the *egla arufa*, "the ritual of the decapitated calf:" If a dead traveler is found between two towns, the elders of both towns must proclaim their people clean from the crime of neglect that might have caused the traveler's death. In traditional societies, the rich and powerful have obligations; the poor have no entitlements.

Modernity—the welfare state—inverted that calculus. In today's world, those less well off feel entitled rather than grateful while the rich and powerful feel no sense of obligation. In fact, tax rates around the world almost guarantee the extinguishment of obligation. Many faiths embraced the concept of tithing—giving a tenth of your income to priests, governments, or the poor. Today, governments claiming to represent the common good often reap over 40% of income. Having already handed over more than four tithes to the common good, what further obligations might possibly remain? Today's taxpayers are far more "generous" than the most charitable residents of the pre-modern world. Yet the mechanism of paying coercive taxes provides none of the spiritual payback of charity. On the other side of the equation, government programs provide far more generously than any historic charity—while depriving the entitled recipients of the spiritual benefits of gratitude.

A society in which the rich feel no obligations and the poor feel no gratitude robs both rich and poor of critical spiritual opportunities. The rich resent what's been taken from them; the poor resent the gap between what they've been handed and the full amount to which they feel entitled. Multiple sets of deep spiritual needs go unmet.

It gets worse. Modern abundance has also brought us atomization. From electric lights to radio to TV to cable to streaming video to VR, each new generation of entertainment technology has permitted us to retreat further and further into isolation. A ballroom must be filled with music capable of appealing to multiple dancers. Headphones need appeal only to an audience of one. We lose the ability to negotiate and to share. We retreat ever further into our own worlds.

Customization exacerbates the situation. We've become so accustomed to environments tailored to our unique tastes that we've lost the ability to deal with even the most minor of disappointments. How often do we sit in rooms sweltering or shivering, angered that whoever was in charge of the thermostat set it at a level two-to-five degrees away from optimal? How often do we ponder that we must be very spoiled to think that we're entitled to room temperatures set at whatever level we might consider ideal for the moment?

Is it any wonder that today's youth—raised on customization—cower at exposure to uncomfortable ideas? How dare a stray utterance, thought, or concept enter my space? I've tailored that space to suit my unique tastes! I feel safe here! No need to compromise, no consideration to others, nothing! It's a space in which I reign supreme! And you have soiled it with an utterance that clashes with the décor! By what right? Nor, by the same logic, is it surprising that their customization has reached into their own bodies to promote an era of customized gender identity.

Delving once again into the language of science, research on the limbic system posits that part of the mammalian brain develops connections between individuals. It explains why a dog may love its master in ways that a lizard cannot. The reptilian brain knows only the self. There is an internal world and an external world. Other lizards—not to mention humans—are simply parts of the environment. No lizard has ever felt lonely because another lizard departed or died. Many reptiles eat their own young without so much as a pang of guilt. Not so with mammals. We mammals develop attachments. We feel connections. We individualize those connections to specific others. We miss them when they are gone. We love. As the species blessed with the most sophisticated mammalian brains, we feel those things most acutely. Yet our marvelous technological advances have taken them from us.

Abundance, atomization, and customization are starving our limbic systems. Our deep need for connection is increasingly unmet. It's no surprise that abundance feeds depression. Whether cast in the language of psychology, biology, or spirituality, the message is the same: Life is far richer when lived with other people. No material abundance can compensate for the loss of connection. Yet the more materiality we accumulate, the less connected we become.

Traditional faiths all understand the challenge. They provide at least partial solutions to the faithful. They have been stymied, however, at reaching those who have rejected their traditional language and metaphor.

Wokeism has reached those people. It has not, however, offered any solution to this fundamental spiritual challenge of our time. The Achilles heel of Wokeism is that far from confronting disconnection, it embraces it. Wokeism welcomes the entitled disconnection of its flock. It can bring people together in a room or on a social network, but it can never bind them. Its commitment to letting each adherent find a distinct truth eliminates the core concept of community.

At the end of the day, Wokeism cannot possibly address the deepest and most central spiritual needs of today's anti-traditionalist elites. It will fail as a faith notwithstanding the potential appeal of its various components. The question that remains open, however, is whether our traditional faiths can find ways to attract the elites to whom Wokeism appears most attractive.

16. Reality Makes Sense

Early in this inquiry I posed a question that far too few authors seem willing to pose: Why listen to me? We've now reached the point where I pose the follow up: What am I missing? I'm hardly the first to ponder the rise of Wokeism and its implications to the American future. Many people have tried to make sense of Wokeism, both holistically and in each of its parts. Far too many of them end up identifying some form of mass psychosis or far-reaching conspiracy.

I'm not a fan of such explanations. Insanity explains everything and thus nothing. The same is true of conspiracy theories. Yet while large conspiracies are rare, mass movements are common. Large numbers of people often come to believe the same thing quite quickly. Examples of mass movements include religions, political and economic ideologies, investment bubbles, fashions, styles, and pop culture trends. Some of those mass movements are extraordinarily durable, lasting centuries or millennia. Others come and go in weeks. Either way, they represent a widely held set of shared beliefs capable of directing individual behavior and the course of history notwithstanding the difficulty that many believers would encounter if asked to explain or justify their beliefs.

How does that happen? I start with two core hypotheses. First, people respond rationally to the incentives before them. Second, reality makes sense. If something happened, it happened for a reason. If many people suddenly adopt the same belief and begin to act upon it, the key to understanding the phenomenon likely lies in the adopters' incentives.

When I see things happening that I don't understand—and that happens a lot—I make certain assumptions about the people driving them. I assume that both the key players and their mass followers are rational. As someone who has studied rational decision-making, I like to back out the two key components of each decision. In the technical language of Bayesian analysis, they're probability and utility. In casual conversation, they translate into beliefs and values. Stated simply, when you—or anyone else—chooses to do one thing over another, you base your decisions on both your beliefs about what is likely to follow your action and upon the values you bring to the table.

Now, we all make plenty of decisions without recourse to rational decision-making. We act impulsively and emotionally and try to justify our actions after the fact. So I'm always willing to accept that any specific individual decision violated the rules of rational decision-making. But— and this point is important—I don't like applying such excuses to two categories of decisions: The first is those that emerge from the aggregate behavior of many people acting independently. Such aggregates define mass movements that I need to understand. The second place I reject irrationality is within the set of decisions that serious people make after considerable deliberation and consultation. In those cases, I assume that the decision-makers considered every reasonably foreseeable consequence of their actions and deemed the mixture of likely costs and benefits wholly worthwhile. I then launch an inquiry into the set of values that would make such a decision rational.

What that means in the context of contemporary Wokeism is that I respect the Woke too much to write them off even when the things they're saying seem to make no sense. And—as we have seen—the Woke say plenty of things that make no apparent sense. Here in the real world, boys can't become girls (and vice versa). Climate change will not end the world within the next few decades. A respiratory ailment with an infection-fatality rate far below 1% is not a plague of Biblical proportions. Masks designed to filter out large particles are ineffective against much smaller particles. The United States is not facing epidemic levels of racist cops killing black men. White supremacism is a fringe movement capable of causing real damage but with a minimal following and less power. Millions of ballots circulating for weeks without custodial supervision cannot be used in credible elections. Science is rarely dispositive—and cannot possibly know anything about the long-term effects of either a newly-discovered virus or a newly-developed vaccine. Terrorists who rape women, slaughter babies, and mutilate corpses are not noble fighters for liberation and justice. The list is long. Those are just selected Woke absurdities that have dominated headlines over the past few years.

That's precisely what bothers me. How could so many smart, educated, seemingly informed people believe such nonsense? Clearly— and it really is quite clear—I must be missing something. What is it? Do they possess values very different from my own? Or do they place very different probabilities on potential scenarios for the future than I do?

Those are excellent questions (if I do say so myself). It's been years since I concluded that what was roiling this country was not a policy debate—which I'm old enough to recall from the twentieth century—but a values conflict. Having spent most of my life in the rarefied affluent, credentialed, professional enclaves of deep blue New York, Los Angeles, San Francisco, and Washington, I was disturbed at how many of the people I'd known and loved seemed comfortable spouting hateful, racist, dangerous irrationalities. Where were they getting them? I had to understand the phenomenon—for my own sanity, if for no other reason. Those questions drove me deep into the study of Wokeism.

I didn't fall into the study of Wokeism casually or happily. I'd spent decades proclaiming it silly to vote on cultural issues when economics and national security were so clearly more important. But I needed to understand what was happening to the people around me. The garbage I heard them spewing was causing me severe emotional pain. Their social media postings were destroying too many of my days. Over the years, the mystery deepened. What began as a casual musing that their commitment to selected apparent insanities was assuming a religious fervor became a theory. And as a theory, I set out to test it using the only two tests that really matter. Does it explain what has happened? Does it predict things before they happen?

My theory passed both tests. By the early 2020s, Wokeism had well-developed notions of pervasive evil (systemic racism), original sin (1619's slavery), the soul (transgenderism), the hierarchy of suffering (intersectionality), end times (apocalyptic global warming), affirmative justice (equity), retributive justice (antiracist discrimination), the clergy (credentialed experts and prestigious bureaucrats), a community-forging challenge (Covid), religious garb with semi-magical properties (face masks), impurity (positive PCR tests), rites of passage (Covid vaccines), untouchables (the unvaxed), purification rituals (quarantine plus negative test), virtue (the common good), saintly martyrs (George Floyd), and myriad other religious parallels.

The notion that government—the font of wisdom and coordinator of the common good—could confer spiritual goods was also in play among the Woke. The Supreme Court's 2015 *Obergefell* decision did far more than legalize gay marriage across the country—a position I'd favored for two decades as a matter of pro-family if nontraditional public policy even while arguing that it was badly miscast as a question of human rights. Justice Kennedy declared civil marriage—a government license, governmental recognition, and government-granted privileges—as a mark of "dignity." When Justice Thomas noted in dissent that dignity is an essential component of our humanity, not something that government can confer or withhold, the Woke erupted in outrage.

Their debate was instructive. From a strictly legal perspective, it's incomprehensible. Dignity is not a legal construct; it exists only in the metaphysical realm. Thomas articulated the traditional view long considered universal (and that had driven my insistence that human rights were not in play): Dignity is an immutable divine gift, conferred when God created Adam "in the image of God." Kennedy articulated the view of contemporary Wokeism: Nothing is innate, divine, or immutable. The government ministers to our spiritual needs as much as it does to our material needs. Implicit in that position is a dismissal of both the "image of God" and "inalienable rights," two central pillars of the American spiritual platform.

What the government confers, the government can withhold. It was thus hardly surprising that the moment the Great Plague descended upon us, governments around the world decreed that no human rights were innate. The concept of natural law underpinning America's civic religion was tossed on the trash heap of history. In times of declared emergency—declared by executive fiat with little-to-no public input, deliberation, or debate—individual freedom collapsed from inalienable rights into government grants. Governments throughout the Anglosphere—the UK, Canada, Australia, New Zealand, the U.S., and most American states—where the tradition of rights vested in natural law was strongest, simply collapsed into Woke autocracies overnight.

A partial selection of the "rights" that evaporated at the whim of designated bureaucrats included: The freedom of speech, the press, religious exercise, assembly, association, petition, privacy, and bodily autonomy; security from warrantless search; due process, equal protection, legal stability, and the rule of law; the right to property; and even the election integrity necessary to secure the republic. Once suspended, governments then meted these rights back out incrementally, easing a bit here while pulling back there, attempting to move slowly enough to declare a "new normal" without triggering widespread backlash and revolution.

These were all obvious and clear violations of the American Spirit— not to mention the law. Granted, not all of those rights are in the Bill of Rights, and that uniquely American document isn't binding anywhere else, but the innate nature of those human rights has always been the animating characteristic of the Anglosphere. Ever since a group of nobles forced King John to sign the Magna Carta in 1215, we've accepted that there are some rights so central to our very being that no government can infringe them legitimately.

No more. That old-style concept emerged from an Americanism rooted in the Bible. Wokeism grows from entirely distinct roots. Human rights and freedoms—of any sort—mean that some individuals must be allowed to make selfish decisions running counter to the common good. Ethical Wokeism rejects that formulation. Under Wokeism, freedom exists only within acceptable boundaries. That's a fairly standard formulation in authoritarian societies.

No surprise then that, as the religious/spiritual model of Wokeism predicted, the Woke began establishing their faith the moment they took power. Their shock troops seized the streets of numerous American cities, chanting angry Woke pieties that none were allowed to question. Fawning Woke reporters gushed about their bravery, using arson fires as backdrops for their declarations about peace, justice, fairness, and the common good. Those with the temerity to suggest that perhaps vandalism and lynch mobs were incompatible with justice were vilified—and rightly so. After all, they were promoting an obsolete, "debunked" form of justice rooted in the systemically racist, biblically based, American civic religion. Municipal codes and election laws changed repeatedly, overnight, at the whims of bureaucrats who simply claimed the right to change them. Even the pretense of ballot integrity evaporated. Any intimation that perhaps circulating tens of millions of ballots, freely, without any custodial supervision or fixed rules concerning handling, delivery, or tabulation, might compromise the credibility of the election was derided as racist.

Why? Because in the Woke deconstruction of the term, it was. The entirety of American spirituality, the human rights it worshipped as innate, the security of its citizenry, and the election processes designed to protect them, were all elements of the pre-Woke status quo. And that status quo, as the Woke constantly remind us, was pungent with original sin and constructed to perpetuate exploitation.

In the world of facts, history, logic, scientific inquiry, open debate, and rationality it was all nonsensical. Which is fine, because Wokeism rejects every one of those attributes as racist manifestations of "white" imperialism. In the deconstructed realm of Wokeism, it was all Gospel Truth. The only real question the Woke faced was what to do about it.

By the end of 2020, Wokeism faced a major challenge: How could it best deploy its enormous power to destroy those who continued to cling bitterly to outdated Biblical morality, traditional religions, and the American spirit?

The history of religion contains many useful lessons. Wokeism was hardly the first new faith to find itself ascendant among a population that was less than fully on board. How had past faiths defended their Truths against the scurrilous lies of the irredeemably evil reactionaries? Fortunately for the Woke, the most directly applicable historical lessons are entirely consistent with Wokeism. If bad people are going to say or print things designed to mislead those the Woke seek to convert, well, THERE OUGHT TO BE A LAW AGAINST THAT!!! There's a name for such laws: Anti-blasphemy.

The world has never had any shortage of anti-blasphemy laws. They exist, in explicit form, in many parts of the world still subject to a dominant religion blurring the lines among faith, lifestyle, society, and culture. In recent decades, Islamists running the Organization of the Islamic Conference (OIC) have sought to internationalize their anti-blasphemy laws using the misleading term "Islamophobia." Islamist organizations and communities throughout the Western world have attempted to import them. Those attempts have proved controversial everywhere, for the simple reason that the West did away with anti-blasphemy laws centuries ago. The illegality of questioning, challenging, undermining, deriding, or even mocking the beliefs or practices of a faith is incompatible with the ethos that has dominated Western life for a very long time.

Anti-blasphemy laws are explicitly counter to the American Spirit. The right to reject religion is inherent in the free exercise of religion. And the minute you reject a religion, the elements of that religion requiring faith begin to look a little silly. Every faith embodies beliefs whose justifications lie beyond the narrow realms of facts, history, logic, scientific inquiry, open debate, and rationality. Wokeism is hardly the first religion to demand that its adherents see beyond the narrow realities of the physical world. In fact, belief in metaphysical specifics in the absence of dispositive evidence is the essence of "faith." In that respect, Wokeism is far more typical than the American Spirit. Jefferson's introduction of America's ethically based civic religion was uniquely honest on that account: *We* hold these truths to be self evident. Look down Jefferson's list of allegedly self-evident truths. Try validating them as self-evident using pre-1776 facts, history, logic, scientific inquiry, open debate, and rationality. At best, you'll show that they were good ideas worth trying. They weren't remotely self-evident.

"We hold these Truths" is a pretty good description of the core particularistic beliefs of every faith. It doesn't take much to figure out that indiscriminate murder is detrimental to societal stability. That's why the prohibition on murder is more-or-less universal. Try using only logic and science to derive God's impregnation of a virgin to bring to earth his only son, whose own death on the cross would atone for the sins of humanity. It can't be done. As a 2000-year-old faith, however, Christianity has matured to the point that (at least most of) today's Christians understand that though such faith may be central to their lives, those who lack that faith are not a threat. Wokeism, as a young and immature religion, shows far less self-confidence.

The Woke campaign against "misinformation" cannot be understood in any context other than an anti-blasphemy campaign. Even a quick perusal of the topics labeled "misinformation" shows an abusive deconstruction of the term. There has been no campaign to remove or censor incorrectly stated facts. People, even on social media, remain entirely free to claim that the earth is flat, that gravity is a myth, or that we can breathe underwater. People can defame former lovers or business partners knowing that the barons of social media will take no action unless and until some court orders them to act. People, even on social media, can spin fabricated scurrilous rumors about celebrities or organizations deemed enemies of Wokeism—or of traditional oppressors unworthy of protection, like Jews, Christians, men, or "white people." Such things, it seems, do not qualify as misinformation.

The only alleged "misinformation" ever targeted calls Woke pieties into question. Perhaps you think that the world would have been better off advocating early treatment of Covid rather than isolation and vaccination? Misinformation! What if you have testimonials, studies, or data tending to support your point? Still misinformation! What if you just like to wonder how "scientists" know the long-term safety profile of a newly invented, incompletely tested vaccine? Misinformation! Or suppose you wonder whether all of those unsupervised ballots might have made a difference to the outcome of the 2020 election? Misinformation! Notice that the sainted Dr. Fauci made inconsistent statements? Misinformation! Have an opinion that masking children for two-plus years is abusive? Misinformation! Think that hundreds of protests spreading anarchy and arson down America's main streets were a greater threat than some poorly behaved trespassers on Capitol Hill? Misinformation!

All such things must be banned from public discourse. Why? Because they might lead the weak-minded astray. That's *precisely* the justification for all anti-blasphemy laws.

What's more, even the mechanisms Wokeism has put in place to police such blasphemy have a long history. In Tudor England, the mercantile economy operated through a series of Royal Charters. The Crown would choose a monopolist to run each industry. That monopolist could then grant sublicenses but remained responsible for the functioning of its chartered industry. A group called The Stationers Company held the charter for printing and publishing. Its primary job as the sole authorized printer and publisher in all of England was to ensure that nothing blasphemous ever appeared in print. If it slipped, heads could roll (literally).

Fast forward to the 2020s as Congressional committees pressure social network CEOs to police anti-Woke "misinformation" appearing on their platforms. Or even better, look to April 2022. During that month alone, Elon Musk announced plans to buy, redirect, and open speech on Twitter. Ex-President Obama gave a speech on the importance of fighting misinformation. President Biden announced the formation of America's first ever Disinformation Governance Board, set within the Department of Homeland Security, and led by a devoutly Woke activist.

In the months following Musk's takeover of Twitter (since renamed X), the Twitter Files provided overwhelming evidence of censorship, propaganda, and government moving against its own citizens—largely but not entirely in the defense of Woke pieties. The Woke media ignored the story. Do most Americans understand how tenuous their "God-given" rights remain in the age of ascendant Wokeism? Seems unlikely. After all, warning them about that very real, very imminent threat would be misinformation capable of leading them astray.

The abortive Disinformation Board should have served as a widespread wakeup call. It didn't. The impossibility of squaring a commitment to free speech and a free press with a government-run bureau empowered to differentiate falsehoods from truth incensed far too few Americans. To the Woke, the Bill of Rights is little more than a problematic set of imperialist rules designed to entrench a racist status quo; a Disinformation Board would be an attempted solution. To too many others, a Disinformation Board would have been just one more government bureaucracy they could ignore unless and until it created some personal problem.

The mere idea that a sitting American President could ever forward such a proposal, much less move to make it a reality, is shocking. Not enough Americans were shocked. The elite power structure of the United States has abandoned the American Spirit. The U.S. dropped all pretense of being either a free society or a constitutional republic in March 2020. What we have experienced since then is an elite oligarchy attempting to establish Wokeism as the official faith of the United States. The authoritarians are working to entrench their power and glide into totalitarianism. Should they succeed, they will hardly be history's first.

Benjamin Franklin famously said that America's founders had handed us a republic, if we could keep it. We've had a good run. "Congress shall make no law respecting an establishment of religion?" Not a problem. The Woke insist that theirs is not a religion even as they move to establish it. Present trends are largely favorable for their success.

The reality all makes sense if you ask the right questions. That's the best indication that the questions you're asking are the right ones. It helps if you have the courage to face even deeply uncomfortable answers.

17. A Decent Respect to the Opinions of Mankind

Sometimes a little diversion is in order. To this point, nearly everything we've discussed has been about America. Yet just as no man is an island, neither is any country. While we're mired in a spiritual crisis that seems to be verging on an all-out religious war, the rest of the world is hardly sitting still. As Thomas Jefferson noted in the Declaration's preamble, "a decent respect to the opinions of mankind" is pretty important. Few of the trends hitting America are localized. The conflict between tradition and modernity is a defining feature of our time, not of our country. The shift from scarcity to abundance may have begun in the West, but it's since gone global. Every nation, every society, every institution, every faith, and every ideology has had to address it. American responses didn't arise in a vacuum. They influence, are influenced by, and interact with other responses to the same phenomena. So let's take a bit of a world tour.

Wokeism, as we've been discussing, is by far the greatest internal threat to the American Spirit. Because America is unique even among Western nations, the Woke threat has manifested itself differently elsewhere. That's perhaps clearest in looking at some of the differences between its status in the U.S. and the EU. Apocalyptic climate change plays a far larger role in European politics than in the U.S. As a result, it's been far more toxic. It already threatens to curtail German energy and Dutch farming. It's devastated once-promising nuclear industries and heightened reliance on Russian oil and gas—then crippled even the mighty German economy when that reliance was severed in a pique of sanctions and sabotage.

Overall, while the Woke climate apocalypse may have become an article of faith among the European elite, it lacks much of the theological edge that appeals to its American adherents. The difference is even clearer when looking at transgender issues; even the proudly Woke French recognize that America's Woke push to mutilate and sterilize children is insane and bestial. When it came to Covid extremism, Sweden—and to a lesser extent, the rest of Scandinavia—led the world in rational responses.

These differences are not terribly surprising. American spiritual traditions and religious history assumed their own trajectory nearly 500 years ago—while Europe's counterreformation was still raging. When America was founded as a creedal nation, it rested upon a novel spiritual tradition already well over a century old. John Winthrop saw us as a shining city on a hill long before anyone contemplated independence from Great Britain. Europe has had its own complicated relationship with faith and with its own traditions—a relationship that further varies from European country to European country. It's unsurprising that the spiritual juggernaut of Wokeism has played itself out differently in Europe. Woke Europeans may share a great deal with their American counterparts, but they're far less religious and far more willing to downplay the parts of Wokeism that don't feel right. For all its anti-Americanism, contemporary Wokeism is also, in many ways, a very American response to a creedal nation mired in a spiritual crisis.

Wokeism is far less of a force outside the U.S. and the EU. There are, however, two important anti-American global ideologies aligned with Wokeism's destructive goals. The first is Islamism, one of many denominational interpretations of a faith tradition far older than the American Spirit. The second, like Wokeism, derived from the utopian tradition. Deng Xiaoping called it "Socialism with Chinese Characteristics," and though many have questioned its fidelity to socialism, the name is apt. This "Chinese Model" marries the Western utopian tradition to China's historic reverence for centralized control and authority. Islamism and Chinese Communism are both deeply antithetical to America's own spiritual roots. Not surprisingly, Wokeism has allied with both in its drive to displace and supplant America.

Before digging a bit deeper, it's important to recall that this entire inquiry is focused on the American nation and the animating spirit that makes it exceptional. While all such inquiries overlap with a consideration of the interests of the United States, the two are not synonymous. After all, the U.S. government is merely something "instituted among men" to secure the rights at the center of our American spiritual traditions. It's entirely possible for a foreign power to challenge the security or economic interests of the U.S. without threatening to undermine the spiritual basis of the American nation.

Vladimir Putin's Russia is perhaps today's most prominent example. Putin's agenda of territorial expansion and economic control of Eastern Europe and Central Asia runs counter to U.S. interests. Putin himself has hardly been bashful about claiming as much. Putin's internal governance of Russia also runs afoul of many truths that we, as Americans, hold to be self-evident. At the same time, however, Putin appreciates quite fully that he is running a government instituted by man with the goal and purpose of securing the central concerns of the Russian nation (as he sees them).

That goal poses no ideological threat to the American nation. Part of recognizing our own uniqueness and exceptionalism is accepting that the world's many other nations hold very different truths to be self-evident. Russian history and tradition, though grounded in the same broad Biblical tradition as our own, are distinct. Whether Putin's governance is true to Russia's traditions is a question for Russians to work out among themselves. Putin exerts little effort trying to persuade the members of other nations (other than those he considers Russian breakaways) that they should be more like Russia. Putin may be expansionist, but he's not evangelical. He understands that Americans are not like Russians, and he's fine with that—as long as we Americans stay out of his way. There's no organized movement—in Russia, in the U.S., or anywhere else—trying to get America to look more like Russia.

Putin's challenges are thus entirely geostrategic and economic threats to U.S. interests, not ideological threats to American values or traditions. The same cannot be said about Islamism and Chinese Communism.

Islamism is by far the highest profile contemporary proof that not every denomination or interpretation of every faith tradition is compatible with Americanism—or can serve as a viable completion to the American spiritual platform. That incompatibility has nothing to do with the Islamic roots of Islamism. It has everything to do with the supremacist roots of Islamism.

It's hard to think of any belief more antithetical to the idea that "all men are created equal" than supremacism. Supremacism starts with the racist belief that there are meaningful and inherent differences among groups. It moves from there to assert that group inequality is real and appropriate; it establishes a pecking order assigning distinct rights and responsibilities to each group. It ends its toxic brew by proclaiming the essential superiority of one group over all others. That supreme group is entitled to rule. All lesser groups must remain subservient and pay homage to their superiors. Universalist supremacists believe that that pecking order, the right to rule, and expectations of homage extend to all people at all times. All Islamists are universalist supremacists; most non-Islamist Muslims are not.

As obviously anti-American as supremacism is, it has hardly been alien to our history. White supremacism was central to slavery and Jim Crow, as well as to immensely powerful organizations like the Ku Klux Klan. Though by the dawn of the twenty-first century we had more-or-less eliminated white supremacism as a significant political, social, or cultural force, it has never disappeared entirely. Today, it persists in the fever corners of the Internet and social media, where it serves as an inspiration to some of society's lost, disturbed, violent misfits.

Wokeism, in its constant drive to defame Americans, has deconstructed "white supremacism" to include all forms of peaceful coexistence with any society whose history includes the taint of actual white supremacism. In other words, pretty much any non-Woke Westerner who does not rail against European and American history qualifies as a white supremacist in the deconstructed Woke lexicon. For present purposes, we'll stick to the actual definition of the term.

White supremacism remains worth noting and tracking, but unless you have the misfortune of a personal encounter with one of America's relatively few bona fide white supremacists, it's unlikely to play much of a role in your life. It's also worth the effort to ensure that it never rises, phoenix-like, from the ashes. No, in America today, the only indigenous supremacist movements of any consequence come from black supremacist groups like Louis Farrakhan's Nation of Islam, the leadership of groups like Black Lives Matter, a handful of other corners of Wokeism—and from Islamists.

At the global level, Islamism is by far the most important and dynamic expression of supremacism. Islamists come in many stripes—including variants of both Sunni and Shiite Islam—and employ many strategies. What they all have in common, however, is the deep certainty that their particular interpretation of Islam makes them superior to the rest of the planet, uniquely suited to rule, and due deference from those who have discovered and embraced enough elements of God's truth to be allowed to live. While they alone constitute the faithful, the planet's many other peoples and faiths fall into two categories: *dhimmis*, who are allowed to live with their errors as long as they accept the faithful as their superiors, and idolators, who must be killed. Muslims who disagree with their particular interpretation of their faith are apostates, similarly marked for death.

Islamists disagree among themselves about numerous theological, strategic, and tactical matters. The Islamic Republic of Iran more-or-less controls all Islamist Shiite movements. It deploys them in the service of global theocratic rule—and a reign of terror until the world reaches it. The Sunni Muslim Brotherhood (*Ikwhan*) engages in the professions, tries to blend into society, and works to undermine institutions of civil society around the world. Its leadership has learned to exhibit strategic patience, and it deploys violence only when useful in achieving a specific goal. Its greatest current patrons are Turkey and Qatar.

The short (2012-13), nasty, and disastrous reign of Egypt's Mohammed Morsi marked the clearest ascendance of the Brotherhood into leadership of a major country, but Brotherhood-linked political parties are popular throughout the Arab world. The terrorist organization Hamas is the Brotherhood's Gaza chapter. Most of the other important Sunni terrorist organizations—starting with the PLO, running through Al Qaeda and ISIS—were founded by former Brothers who rejected their leadership's long-term strategy and preferred acts of spectacular violence. Another important source of Islamist thought is Wahhabism, a movement that originated in the eighteenth-century Arabian Peninsula. In the twentieth century, Saudi Arabia used its oil wealth to spread Wahhabism worldwide. Though current *de facto* Saudi leader Crown Prince Muhammad bin Sultan (MBS) has moved away from this historic alliance with the Wahhabi and curtailed Saudi largesse to Wahhabi institutions, others—notably the current Qatari government—have filled the void.

As an always-supremacist and frequently violent ideology, Islamism is clearly incompatible with the American spirit. Unfortunately, Islamists dominate the leadership of America's most prominent Muslim organizations. That dominance complicates the work of the many Muslims who came to America specifically seeking an Islam fully compatible with America's spiritual platform. It also gives Islam and Muslims a bad reputation in some American circles. Complicating their lives even further, Wokeism has formed a deep alliance with Islamist organizations in America and abroad. The Woke frequently advocate on behalf of Iran, Qatar, Turkey, and the Muslim Brotherhood. Their longstanding love of the Saudis evaporated when MBS turned against Islamism—explaining their burning outrage at the botched Saudi assassination of the Islamist apologist and mouthpiece Jamal Khashoggi. Qatar now funds most Middle East studies institutes at American universities. In return, their Woke professors, students, and graduates continue their longstanding affinity for Islamist groups.

Like many American ethnic, religious, and minority communities, America's Muslims are at the mercy of a dismal leadership uninterested in their welfare. Prominent organizations like the Council on American-Islamic Relations (CAIR) and the Islamic Society of North America (ISNA), as well as many of America's largest and wealthiest mosques, advocate for Islamism—and often against interpretations of Islam fully compatible with Americanism. While they're certainly more presentable, calmer, and less personally violent than many overseas Islamists, they're at least as dangerous—both to American Muslims and to the broader American society.

The Woke embrace of Islamism has turned these Islamists into a serious anti-American force in American politics—beginning with America's most politically successful Islamist, Ilhan Omar. Politics, as they say, makes for strange bedfellows and few are stranger than the alliance of Wokeism and Islamism. This "red/green" alliance has already enjoyed decades as a powerful and rising force in European politics. Anyone who believed that American politics might be exempt had their hopes dashed after October 7th, when America's own red/green alliance emerged in full force. It's a deeply dangerous and violent alliance promoting values hostile to the American Spirit and policies dangerous to American safety, welfare, and domestic harmony. Like the Molotov/Ribbentrop pact uniting fascist Nazis and communist Soviets, it elevates a common interest in defeating the forces of freedom and decency above ideology.

For the most part, this alliance plays weak Woke Westerners as dupes. Islamists are far more committed to their ideology, and far more willing to take personal risks to promote it, than are their soft but angry Woke allies. Islamists despise every important element of the Woke agenda. When and where in power, Islamists execute homosexuals and severely curtail women's rights. They have little commitment to the environment and promote their own blasphemy laws banning much of what the Woke advocate. Islamist supremacism puts even the most outrageous of the Woke supremacists to shame. What they have in common is an abiding anti-Americanism and a burning hatred of both Jews and Christians. In today's world, that's more than enough of a basis for a beautiful friendship.

The world's other leading anti-American ideology, Chinese Communism, may be even more pernicious—in large part because unlike Islamism, it dovetails beautifully with Wokeism. Going back to Deng's original formulation, this model combines quasi-capitalist semi-free markets with authoritarian social controls.

Since its introduction in the 1980s, Deng's model has won many admirers—including much of the American and Western elite. Stripped to its essentials, Socialism with Chinese characteristics promotes innovation, entrepreneurship, and economic growth while nevertheless maintaining government control over large swathes of human behavior. In other words, it's a manifestly unfree system that maintains selected trappings of freedom, particularly in the economic realm.

Over the course of decades, China's Communist elite demonstrated the benefits that social controls of the citizenry confer upon the elites who wield that control "for the common good." Western elites, never too enamored with the selfish, backward, deplorable masses occupying space in their own countries, took notice. Whatever it was that China was doing seemed to be working: China's people were getting richer without getting freer—yet rarely complaining. Inconvenient, inferior, or ideologically questionable citizens were handled easily; many even proved useful as slaves or organ donors.

When China's elites invited Woke Western elites to share the bounties of its growing markets, learn the Chinese system, and appreciate its benefits, Western elites swooned. And why not? Authoritarians like the Chinese Communist Party (CCP) can inflict unpopular policies necessary to "serve the common good" far more easily than can their democratic counterparts. *New York Times* columnist Tom Friedman even wished that the U.S. could be "China for a day," though the logic of his argument suggested that we'd need a day of authoritarianism each time Wokeism identified a new challenge to the common good.

Supremacism, unequal treatment of strong and weak, and sadism are all "characteristics" the CCP wields with efficiency and pride. As long it deploys them effectively, they're not likely to bother the Woke. Wokeism imported many of them, initially gingerly out of concern for a backlash. When the Woke read the 2012 election as giving them license to transform America in their image, however, all bets were off. Their importation of these most important Chinese exports grew increasingly brazen. Since the March 2020 shutdowns, few among the Woke even bother to pretend that constitutional norms, the needs of a free republic, or our inalienable human rights might slow them down. Yes, they like insisting that nothing has changed, but even the efforts expended keeping up appearances have waned with frightening speed.

Recall that by mid-2020, Klaus Schwab was crowing that global government actions taken to combat Covid had "reset" the world's socioeconomic fabric. The new world order, he gushed, would be far more akin to Chinese Communism than to America's founding principles. Fortunately for the world, Schwab had spent decades laying the groundwork to crush civil liberties. He'd been a key contributor to the stakeholder capitalism that has enmeshed so many of our leading corporations in "Environmental, Social, and Governance" (ESG) policies deeply at odds with their fiduciary responsibility to shareholders.

The Chinese Communist Model's threat to America—its nation, its spirit, and its founding ideals—is thus clear and palpable. Wokeism itself is an ideology. It's overtaken our most important cultural institutions, but it will need a distinct strategy to undermine our governance fully. Importation of the Chinese Communist Model via global governance is the most promising route they've found to date. Schwab's books provide the roadmap.

So is all lost? Are we really in it alone? Suppose American Wokeism cuts a deal with China to roll out its governance fully, concedes that as a non-European people the Chinese are probably superior anyway, and turns the U.S. into a totalitarian state that permits prosperity? Suppose Wokeism then joins China in letting Islamists run wild as long as they do it at someone else's party? Suppose the EU continues thinking it can be Woker than Wokeism on climate while holding Woke gender ideology at arms length? Suppose that our sister nations of the Anglosphere—the UK, Canada, Australia, and New Zealand—continue their own rapid descents into Wokeism (albeit in a mix somewhat different from the American denomination)? Where does that leave those of us still committed to America's founding spirit and the faith traditions that complete it so spectacularly? Would we really have no friends left on this planet?

The answer is: No. The American spirit preaches a compelling message. It has resonated around the world for a reason. It's a positive, uplifting, life-affirming spiritual message. Though it manifests itself differently among nations other than our own, it continues to attract adherents. As Woke as host societies may become, many of their people will always answer the calls of America's founding spirit and compatible traditional faiths. The brave people of Iran—chafing beneath nearly forty-five years of Islamist rule—attest to its continued appeal.

It may thus be far from coincidental that the most promising recent development in forging our future alliances arrived from the Middle East. In 2020, in the waning days of the Trump Administration, the White House hosted the signing of the Abraham Accords. The two principals—Israel and the United Arab Emirates (UAE)—forged the first genuinely warm peace in the entire region since the fall of the Ottoman Empire. Several other Arab states signed on quickly; with only a bit of encouragement from the White House, others might do so as well. Those still standing on the sidelines are watching cautiously to see whether Western powers will stand up to the Woke/Islamist mobs roiling their cities and allow Israel to deal the Islamist terrorists of Hamas a death blow. Though none can admit it openly, all Arab leaders focused on the healthy development of their societies are desperate for a decisive Israeli victory.

The Abraham Accords, however, have a significance that transcends the Middle East. Of all the world's countries, few have spent more time aligning tradition with modernity than have Israel and the UAE. These are two societies in which the religious, anti-religious, and even Woke coexist—often uneasily—side-by-side. The hidden message of the Abraham Accords is thus not geopolitical but cultural and spiritual. In the spirit of America's founding, two societies oriented around non-Christian faiths chose a solution similar to the one that Jefferson pioneered in 1776: A basic platform of decency, morality, and coexistence upon which distinctive traditions can provide completion.

Other nations have undergone similar struggles. Central Europe's Visegrad group—Poland, Czechia, Slovakia, and Hungary—is engaged in the challenge of preserving unique national characters amidst a movement towards European harmonization and globalization. Brexit proved that many Brits appreciate the genuine exceptionalism at the heart of the Anglo branch of Western civilization—the branch from which America grew. They understand that it's threatened. They're willing to do the work to preserve it. Austria, Scandinavia, Italy, and the Netherlands have demonstrated inklings of the same. Further abroad, India faces its own challenges reconciling its glorious traditions with the needs of modernity.

None of these nations are American. They're as proud of their own traditions as we are of ours. They understand, however, that Wokeism is incompatible with their own national traditions and their own faith traditions. These nations thus promise to become our greatest allies in our quest to contain the homegrown, anti-American threat of Wokeism.

18. Message to the Faithful

We're nearing the end of our inquiry, which is where it becomes relevant that I'm not a wannabe guru. I lack the wherewithal, the talent, the inspiration, and the sense of self-aggrandizement I'd need to launch a new religion (which, yet again, is something we emphatically do not need). What I am is a professional troubleshooter, problem-solver, and strategist. Which is fortunate, because American society is in serious trouble, facing deep problems, and in dire need of a strategy to right itself before it's too late.

I've tried to tell the stories of America's spiritual crisis, the American Spirit, and the Great Awokening in a way that builds towards a solution. Not that any of these steps are simple, but we've got to do three things: Treat Wokeism like the religion it is. Reinvigorate the American Spirit. Help traditional faiths deploy resonant language and metaphor to address the unspoken spiritual needs of those most in crisis.

The hardest of those tasks, finding the right messages in traditional faiths, is largely out of my purview precisely because I don't want to found my own religion. I'm not a fan of denominations that simply reinvent their faith's beliefs, practices, and traditions to suit the taste of today's parishioners.

I take deep personal offense at the Jewish organizations and clergy that have untethered Judaism from its rich past. Judaism places at its center the unity of God, the nation of Israel, and the eternal covenant linking them together. To Jews, the Torah's designation of the Israelites as a "kingdom of priests and a holy nation" essentially set up a demonstration project. Adherence to God's covenant is supposed to set a model for the rest of the world to follow—a light unto the nations. Judaism doesn't simply morph into whatever it is that enough Jews believe. Jewish laws and rituals have remained largely unchanged for millennia. Jewish positions on controversial topics like abortion, euthanasia, and sexuality were formed long ago—and they do not align with those of Wokeism. Jewish positions on the environment, taxes, welfare, warfare, and countless other matters of contemporary politics are far more flexible; some Woke positions may be consistent with Jewish views, but then so too are many non-Woke positions. The contemporary reduction of Judaism to a bland ethical command to "fix the world" (*tikkun olam*) in a manner that coincidentally aligns perfectly with Wokeism is both offensive and anti-Jewish.

That addresses half the identity I take personally. In the other half, as an American whose personal level of faith and religious observance has varied widely throughout his life, I remain a staunch believer in free will and free choice. I find the notion of enforced observance at least as offensive as the notion of amorphous traditionalism. But an individual choice to transgress or bend one or more religious rules can do nothing to alter the tradition—or the viability of the rules themselves.

Judaism is what it is, regardless of what any number of today's Jews may want it to be. There may be some red lines—in life choices or political choices—that make an individual, even an individual Jew, anti-Jewish (in fact, there almost certainly are such red lines). But traditionalists must take pains to ensure that the lines they identify are few, clear, and necessary to preserve the continued existence or safety of the Jewish people—the right and the practical ability of Jews to live as Jews—not simply those that run against the Jewish practice of the individual. The same is true of Christianity, Islam, and all other traditional faiths.

Beyond that, by all means, let people know when Judaism expects something of them. If they choose to live, act, or vote differently—well, that's the American Spirit in action. It's also, however, the *American* component of American Judaism that has allowed Judaism and Jews to thrive in America. No one ever guaranteed that America would permit every traditional interpretation of every faith. Religious traditionalists of all stripes were invited to find, define, or tailor versions of their traditions to American soil. That task was always going to be easier for some than for others. The invitation remains as it was. I've presented this inquiry in part as a call to America's traditional faith leaders to remember that invitation and its terms, to look in the mirror, and to see what needs to be done to accept it within contemporary American sociological context.

I use the example of Judaism only because as *my* faith, it's the only one I take personally. But I come to the table showing the same respect, assessments, and expectations for other faiths. From what I can see of American Christianity, denominations anchored in Christian traditions and practices remain deeply Christian. Those committed to chasing the tastes of their parishioners are sliding into Wokeism. I would be surprised to learn that any other American faiths have avoided this pattern. America's Muslims also face the opposite challenge. Too many of their organizations and leaders are committed to Islamism, a supremacist interpretation inherently incompatible with the American Spirit. A viable American Islam must turn sharply against that leadership and instead find inspiration among other schools of contemporary Islamic thought.

When I say that I'm reaching out to America's faith leaders, I'm looking primarily towards leaders willing to ask something of their flocks—yet limit their demands to those consistent with the American spiritual platform upon which they must grow. Only those who make such demands have anything real to offer. Only those anchored in the American Spirit can be part of the solution. Only those anchored to their own traditions can lead; those who chase the latest trends and tastes are merely followers. The challenge these traditionalist leaders face—as always—is to meet adherents where they are and to show them how traditional anchors address their needs.

That's tough work. To what extent will it require new approaches? Clearly, any traditionally anchored denomination or community that has made it this far has been doing something right. The landscape is replete with the shells of once-proud churches. On the other hand, it's hard to miss the popularity of the less-demanding denominations, the rise of the religious "nones," or the widespread subscriptions to Marxism, Wokeism, and other variants of utopianism—particularly among the educated professional elite. Those movements serve as stark rebukes, testaments to the failure of traditional faiths to reach so many. The only fair, objective assessment of America's traditionalist leaders is that they've been doing some things right and some things wrong. That leaves ample room for improvement.

America's traditional faith leaders must reach deep into their own traditions to find ways to reach their lost sheep—those grappling with abundance rather than scarcity, those whose unarticulated spiritual needs can be met only in the language of the mundane.

If I knew how to meet that challenge, I might change my mind and become a guru after all. I don't. I know that many of our finest faith leaders have been trying. If you're one of them, I'm speaking to you. Perhaps the materials that I've laid out here can provide some assistance.

Recognize which of your traditions are best attuned to the concerns surrounding abundance: Fear of slipping back into scarcity; guilt about having produced too much garbage; the goal of distributing the bounty to those in need; and dread that some cosmic force will punish us for our hubris.

Teach that true concerns about distribution and equality must emphasize access and opportunity, not outcome, because only the former are achievable.

Help the skeptical connect with sources of soul, inner truth, good, and evil. Remind them of the value of connectedness and community.

Impress upon them their debts to the faith without making them feel worthless when they fail—or choose to opt out of specifics.

Do all of those things without compromising commitment to your own traditions and America can experience a spiritual revival in full partnership with the American Spirit.

That brings us to the task of reinvigorating an American Spirit in deep need of reinvigoration. Sadly, several generations of American leadership have let it become moribund. Few today even remember what it once was.

Our inquiry is thus not the only thing that appears to be nearing its end. The country that once embodied the American Spirit has slipped into history. The United States today is neither a constitutional republic nor a free society. It is a bureaucratic elitist oligarchy that fails the primary test of legitimacy it laid out for itself: It neither recognizes nor secures our inalienable liberties. Fortunately, the American Spirit has been battered rather than beaten. It's far from dead. A republican restoration is possible —but only if we work towards it.

So before wrapping up entirely, let's take an honest if unconventional look at our history—modeled after a country that, at least in this respect, has been far more honest about its history than has our own: France. When Americans first declared independence in 1776, France was an absolute monarchy. Since then, it's cycled through four republics, two empires, a restored absolute monarchy, a constitutional monarchy, and a fascist puppet state. It's now in its fifth republic, which it honestly calls the Fifth French Republic.

We've been remiss in our own labeling. Though few Americans like to admit it, we've changed regimes more than once. The revolutionary period and the Articles of Confederation (1776-89) gave the world the First American Republic. It failed. The Constitution of 1789 gave birth to a far more robust Second American Republic. That one collapsed into secession and civil war in 1860. The post-civil war Constitutional Amendments and deletions yielded a Third American Republic with very different takes on equality, citizenship, and the rights of states from the Second.

That Third Republic ended not with a bang, but a whimper. No one ever announced that it was over or took a dramatic step to end it. Instead, the protracted rise of the administrative state from Woodrow Wilson to Lyndon Johnson morphed it into something very, very different. It's likely impossible to put a date on the demise of the Third American Republic and the rise of the Fourth, but most Americans alive today have known only that Fourth American Republic.

Our Fourth Republic was always problematic—large parts of it seemed to lack clear Constitutional bases—but it always embraced the notion of fundamental rights. In fact, one of the harshest consistent critiques against it was the creativity it put into finding new rights to remove from the political process. Its sanctification of inalienable rights was thus at least partial compensation for its casual attitude towards the written Constitution. The last vestiges of that republican virtue, however, died when our leadership dropped all pretense of honoring certain rights as inalienable in March 2020. The "Covid emergency" declaration and the measures it justified were more than incompatible with the Bill of Rights. They buried the entire American idea.

That's not hyperbole. Go back to March 2020 and consider what happened. What was the "emergency?" In March 2020, the U.S. was experiencing neither widespread death nor widespread disease. Hospitals reported no capacity issues. But thanks to the government, press reports, and information fed from foreign powers and NGOs that do not necessarily have our best interests at heart, people—including a supermajority of

Americans—were terrified. Widespread panic motivated allegedly reasonable people to behave unreasonably. Contra JFK, the call went out to pay any price, bear any burden, meet any hardship, sacrifice any liberty, censor any dissent, in the struggle against a viral respiratory disease.

In response to that panic, the federal government and most of the states engaged in the most comprehensive suppression of civil liberties in America history. The moment that happened, a precedent was set. From March 2020 on forward, if the government determines that enough Americans are sufficiently frightened (or should be sufficiently frightened), the government may suspend any and all civil liberties. So much for the idea that these rights are inalienable and that the only proper and legitimate role of government is to secure them.

The few governors who realized the error early and moved to correct it quickly deserve immense credit for standing against the crowd, but their efforts were too little too late to avoid having set the precedent. In March 2020, when the initial lockdowns began, there was not a single prominent American political leader in either party willing to state simply, clearly, and loudly that the proposed suppression of civil liberties was entirely incompatible with the American idea.

As a result, in America today as across the globe, there are no inalienable rights. Period. The idea that motivated the great American experiment reigns nowhere. It was a fine idea that brought enormous benefits to the world, but it was the primary casualty of Covid. The American Spirit remains alive, though on life support, far from the halls of power. If we can revive it, we can restore America's historic republicanism—breathing life into a Fifth American Republic. If not, well, as France has shown, there will likely still be a United States. It may be smaller or even larger—we've changed our map and our flag many times since 1776. It may continue to feign democracy, concede that it's an elitist oligarchy, or slide into fully totalitarian rule. It may be Woke or utopian or something else. It will not, however, be the embodiment of the American nation forged in the 1776 Declaration.

A successful reinvigoration of the American Spirit, in turn, would give salience to the final task: What would it mean for Wokeism to become but one of the many religions capable of providing completion to the

American spiritual platform?

Clearly, if Wokeism is ever to play that role, it will have to mature. Today's Wokeism is supremacist, anti-Biblical, and often violent. It revels in embedding its idiosyncratic beliefs into American institutions, then insisting that all other beliefs are hateful, ignorant, or both. It imposes Woke morality into the parenting and educational practices of non-Woke families and schools. It seeks to become the Established Religion of the United States.

It's unclear that any other variants of Wokeism currently exist. That situation need not persist. People whose faith drives them to wear face masks need not impose their will on others. Woke individuals who advocate racial or ethnic discrimination should be as free to voice their views as are any other racists—while the rest of us strive for a decent, colorblind, "content of character" society. Should Wokeism formalize its gender-declaration rituals, Woke parents finding legal impediments to full participation in those rituals would deserve the same right to sue under the Free Exercise Clause as do adherents of other faiths; the Courts would then have to determine whether the challenged restriction serves an important government objective in the least restrictive manner.

The key to Wokeism's maturation into an American-compatible religion is a strong and clear rejection of Woke supremacism—not because it's Woke but because it's supremacist. The American Spirit—the spiritual platform in the Constitution and the legal treatment of religion embodied in the First Amendment—has proven robust in securing the rights of adherents of many, many faiths. America can never countenance supremacists—of any faith. If the Woke choose to relinquish their war against the American Spirit and instead adapt to live within it, they should be as welcome as were all who came before them. Late nineteenth century American law contained shameful provisions designed to prevent the spread of Mormonism and of Catholicism—representing a mixture of rank bigotry and fear of extremist elements. Yet the ancient faith of Catholicism was able to Americanize and the then-young faith of Mormonism was able to mature. Today, no decent, rational person questions their full compatibility with the American Spirit. The same could become true of a mature, anti-supremacist Wokeism.

Of course, even the mere articulation of such a humble, mature Wokeism highlights how much Woke thinking will have to evolve to become compatible with American ideals. Like all new faiths, Wokeism devotes enormous energy to attacking the old-time religions it claims to have supplanted—for the Woke, that means anything grounded in the Bible. It will be difficult, though perhaps not impossible, for Wokeism to shed its deep antisemitic and anti-Christian bigotries. Wokeism will also have to drop its call for a global empire imposing strict Woke edicts on the masses while exempting the Woke elite—or at the very least, recast that dream as something that will arrive only following some sort of eschatological deliverance.

For all of its grounding in abundance and modernity, that Woke desire for a global Woke empire is a pretty common—and pretty regressive—goal among ascendant totalitarian imperialists. In fact, it was the dominant view almost everywhere until a handful of radical innovators embraced a new set of ideas they amusingly chose to label "self evident" and create an intentionally incomplete spiritual platform.

That American Spirit was a genuine disruption in world history. It created myriad paths for societal improvement. It's well worth preserving. Yet in today's world, it's hanging by a thread. The choice we face is stark. We can reinvigorate the American Spirit and give birth to a Fifth American Republic—or we can glide aimlessly until we morph into something very different, on current trends likely something very Woke. What lies in the American future? The American Spirit or The Great Awokening. One or the other. The choice is ours. May we find the inspiration to make the right choice.

There's nothing ailing America that a little faith couldn't cure. May God bless America—and may America return to blessing God.

Amen.

APPENDIX:
THE AMERICAN SPIRITUAL PLATFORM

They key to describing a spiritual platform is laying out shared core elements that different faiths and denominations can complete in different ways. Any denomination comfortable with the platform can provide a fully American completion. Denominations incompatible with parts of it are incompatible with America.

The following represents the spiritual platform I have teased out of America's founding documents: The Declaration of Independence in its entirety, including the enumeration of grievances; and the Constitution, specifically the Emoluments Clause (Article I, Section 9, Clause 8), the Privileges and Immunities Clause (Article IV, Section 2), the Guarantee Clause (Article IV, Section 4), the Bill of Rights (Amendments 1-10), the post-Civil War Amendments (13-15), and the 24th Amendment on voting rights. It appears most eloquently in the speeches and writings of Abraham Lincoln and Martin Luther King, Jr.

Though it should probably go without saying, the rules of contemporary discourse compel me to note that my attempt to articulate America's spiritual platform is not intended as a statement of law. It is a statement of foundational beliefs about the relationship among an axiomatic divine source, the divinely conferred natural rights of humanity, and the man-made governments instituted to protect those natural rights.

I.   **America is a distinct and exceptional nation:**

- We Americans form a unique nation. We approach other nations as our equals, respectful of their opinions, values, beliefs, and cultures.

- The shared truths we Americans hold to be self-evident define us as a nation. They are what makes us exceptional among the nations. People who do not share those truths cannot claim to be American.

II.   **The defining beliefs of the American nation are modest, foundational, and axiomatic:**

- Our Creator's natural law endowed both humanity as a whole and every individual human with certain inalienable rights.

- We Americans believe that Our Creator endowed all humans with such rights. While we encourage others to share that belief, we recognize that other nations and people may believe differently.

- Our Creator granted inalienable natural rights only to individuals. Governments are man-made entities existing for the sole purpose of securing those rights. Governments may not legitimately infringe upon natural rights or freedoms.

III.   **Inalienable individual rights under natural law:**

a. **Equality:**

- We are all created equal and entitled to equal dignity without regard to the unequal conditions of our births.

- We accept that equal freedom to pursue life, liberty and happiness will necessarily result in inequalities of circumstances.

- It is illegitimate to recognize any status that establishes permanent immutable inequality, such as slavery or nobility.

- It is illegitimate to designate immutable characteristics as a basis of unequal treatment.

b. **Faith:**

- We are free to arrange our lives and affairs according to the precepts of our faiths.

- We are welcome to persuade others to see the broad wisdom underpinning beliefs derived from our own faiths.

- It is illegitimate to impose the precepts of a faith upon Americans who may not share that faith.

c. Freedom:

- We enjoy freedom of speech, writing, expression, and thought.
- We enjoy freedom of peaceable assembly, petition, and association.

d. Security:

- We are free to make private decisions concerning our bodies, our homes, our correspondence, our property, and our relationships.
- We possess the right of self-defense against individuals, organizations, and the government itself, as well as the right to possess the weaponry necessary to secure that defense.

IV. Law:

- American legal systems must afford due process, equal protection, and strict fidelity to the rule of law.
- Any incursions upon our privacy or our property must comply with the law.
- Criminal law and procedure must be fair and humane.
- Civil law and procedure must apply equally to all parties, including the government.
- If emergency measures ever warrant the temporary suspension of certain rights and freedoms, the declaration of the emergency, the announcement of the suspension, and the particularity of its application must all proceed subject to the rule of law.

V. Government:

- Government is an entirely human creation, put in place solely to secure our individual natural rights. Nothing a government does is sacred.
- Legitimate governments arise and persist with the consent of the governed. Governments that infringe natural rights repeatedly and consistently lose all legitimacy.
- All infringements of our inalienable rights are illegitimate. A pattern of government infringement produces despotism.

- Illegitimate governments fail to provide and enforce clear and comprehensible rules of law, refuse to protect citizens from foreign forces, and set their own agents against the citizenry.

- Citizens have a sacred right and duty to overthrow illegitimate governments and to replace them with a new government that will secure their natural rights.

- The federal nature of the United States reflects and respects the American commitment to diversity of opinion. Different states may enact distinct policies reflective of the beliefs, attitudes, values, and opinions of their own citizens.

VI.   Citizenship:

- Citizenship in the United States is a meaningful concept. Citizens are afforded privileges and responsibilities unavailable to non-citizens.

- The government of each state must recognize and provide equal treatment under its own laws to citizens of every state including it own.

- National governments have obligations towards their own citizens that are greater than, and that take priority over, any obligations they may assume toward the citizens of other sovereign states.

- American governments are obligated to conduct free, fair, secure elections in which all citizens, and only citizens, have a meaningful opportunity to vote for their government representatives.